Focus on WRITING 1

Natasha Haugnes

John Beaumont, Series Editor
Borough of Manhattan Community College
City University of New York

ALWAYS LEARNING

PEARSON

Focus on Writing 1

Pearson Education, 10 Bank Street, White Plains, NY 10606

Staff Credits: The people who made up the *Focus on Writing 1* team, representing editorial, production, design, and manufacturing, are Pietro Alongi, Rhea Banker, Danielle Belfiore, Elizabeth Carlson, Nan Clarke, Aerin Csigay, Dave Dickey, Christine Edmonds, Oliva Fernandez, Barry Katzen, Penny Laporte, Jaime Lieber, Tara Maceyak, Amy McCormick, Barbara Perez, Joan Poole, Debbie Sistino, Jane Townsend, Paula Van Ells, and Adina Zoltan.

The Grammar Presentation charts in *Focus on Writing 1* are adapted from *Focus on Grammar 1, Third Edition,* by Irene E. Schoenberg and Jay Maurer, Pearson Education, White Plains, New York, © 2012.

Cover image: Shutterstock.com
Illustrations: Gary Torrisi
Text composition: ElectraGraphics, Inc.
Text font: New Aster

Library of Congress Cataloging-in-Publication Data
Haugnes, Natasha, 1965–
 Focus on writing. 1 / Natasha Haugnes.
  p. cm.
 Includes index.
 ISBN 0-13-231350-2 — ISBN 0-13-231352-9 — ISBN 0-13-231353-7 — ISBN 0-13-231354-5 — ISBN 0-13-231355-3 1. English language—Textbooks for foreign speakers. 2. English language—Rhetoric—Problems, exercises, etc. 3. Report writing—Problems, exercises, etc. I. Title.
 PE1128.H3934 2011
 428.2—dc22

                                                                          2011014764

PEARSON LONGMAN ON THE **WEB**

Pearsonlongman.com offers online resources for teachers and students. Access our Companion Websites, our online catalog, and our local offices around the world.

Visit us at **pearsonlongman.com**.

Printed in the United States of America
ISBN 10: 0-13-231350-2
ISBN 13: 978-0-13-231350-6

4 5 6 7 8 9 10—V082—16 15 14 13

Contents

To the Teacher iv

To the Student vi

Scope and Sequence xii

UNIT 1   Names 2

UNIT 2   Do-It-Yourself 20

UNIT 3   Food 38

UNIT 4   Clothes 60

UNIT 5   Amazing Nature 80

UNIT 6   Helping Hands 100

UNIT 7   Home Sweet Home 124

UNIT 8   Luck 148

Index 172

To the Teacher

Focus on Writing is a five-level series that prepares students for academic coursework. Each book in the series gives students an essential set of tools to ensure that they master not only the writing process, but also the grammatical structures, lexical knowledge, and rhetorical modes required for academic writing. The series provides an incremental course of instruction that progresses from basic sentences (Book 1) and paragraphs (Books 1–3) to essays (Books 3–5). Grammar presentation and focused grammar practice are correlated to *Focus on Grammar*.

A Process Approach to Writing

Over the past 30 years, the *writing process* approach has become the primary paradigm for teaching writing. As cognitive research shows, writing is a recursive process. When students practice the entire writing process repeatedly with careful guidance, they internalize the essential steps, thereby improving their writing and their confidence in themselves as writers.

Each unit in each book of *Focus on Writing* provides direct instruction, clear examples, and continual practice in the writing process. Students draw on their prior knowledge, set goals, gather information, organize ideas and evidence, and monitor their own writing process. Students write topic-related sentences and use them in a basic paragraph (Book 1); they focus on writing an *introduction*, *body*, and *conclusion* for a paragraph (Books 2–3) or essay (Books 3–5). Whether students are writing a group of related sentences, a paragraph, or an essay, they produce a complete, cohesive piece of writing in *every* unit.

Predictable Step-by-Step Units

Focus on Writing is easy to use. Its predictable and consistent unit format guides students step by step through the writing process.

■ PLANNING FOR WRITING

Students are introduced to the unit theme through an engaging image and high-interest reading. Brainstorming tasks develop critical thinking and serve as a springboard for the unit's writing assignment. Vocabulary building activities and writing tips related to the topic and organizational focus of the unit provide opportunities for students to expand their own writing.

■ STEP 1: PREWRITING

In Book 1, students learn the basics of sentence structure and are encouraged to combine sentences into cohesive paragraphs. They choose between two authentic academic writing assignments, explore their ideas through discussions with classmates, and complete a graphic organizer.

In Books 2–5, students learn the basics of a rhetorical structure (e.g., narration, description, opinion, persuasion, compare-contrast, cause-effect, or problem-solution) and choose between two authentic academic writing assignments. Students explore their ideas through freewriting, share them with classmates, and complete a graphic organizer.

STEP 2: WRITING THE FIRST DRAFT

Explanations, examples, and focused practice help students to prepare for their own writing assignment. Writing tasks guide students through the steps of the writing process as they analyze and develop topic sentences, body sentences, and concluding sentences (Books 1–3) and continue on to draft thesis statements and complete introductions, body paragraphs, and conclusions (Books 3–5). At all levels, students learn how to use transitions and other connecting words to knit the parts of their writing together.

STEP 3: REVISING

Before students revise their drafts, they read and analyze a writing model, complete vocabulary exercises, and review writing tips that they then apply to their own writing. A Revision Checklist tailored to the specific assignment guides students through the revision process.

STEP 4: EDITING

Grammar presentation and practice help students make the connection between grammar and writing. An Editing Checklist ensures students check and proofread their final drafts before giving them to their instructors.

Helpful Writing Tools

Each book in the series provides students with an array of writing tools to help them gain confidence in their writing skills.

- *Tip for Writers* presents a level-specific writing skill to help students with their assignment. The tips include asking *wh-* questions, using conjunctions to connect ideas, identifying audience, using descriptive details, and using pronoun referents.

- *Building Word Knowledge* sections give students explicit instruction in key vocabulary topics, for example, word families, collocations, compound nouns, and phrasal verbs.

- *Graphic organizers* help students generate and organize information for their writing assignment. For example, in Book 1, they fill out a timeline for a narrative paragraph and in Book 3, they complete a Venn diagram for a compare-contrast essay. In the final unit of Books 4 and 5, they use multiple organizers.

- *Sample paragraphs and essays* throughout the units, tied to the unit theme and writing assignments, provide clear models for students as they learn how to compose a topic sentence, thesis statement, introduction, body, and conclusion.

Carefully Targeted Grammar Instruction

Each unit in *Focus on Writing* helps students make the essential link between grammar and writing. The grammar topics for each unit are carefully chosen and correlated to *Focus on Grammar* to help students fulfill the writing goals of the unit.

Online Teacher's Manuals

The online Teacher's Manuals include model lesson plans, specific unit overviews, timed writing assignments, authentic student models for each assignment, rubrics targeted specifically for the writing assignment, and answer keys.

To the Student

Welcome to *Focus on Writing*! This book will help you develop your writing skills. You will learn about and practice the steps in the writing process.

All of the units are easy to follow. They include many examples, models and, of course, lots of writing activities.

Read the explanations on the next few pages before you begin Unit 1.

> Before you begin to write, you need to know what you will write about. A picture, a short reading and a **brainstorming** activity will help you get ideas about a topic.

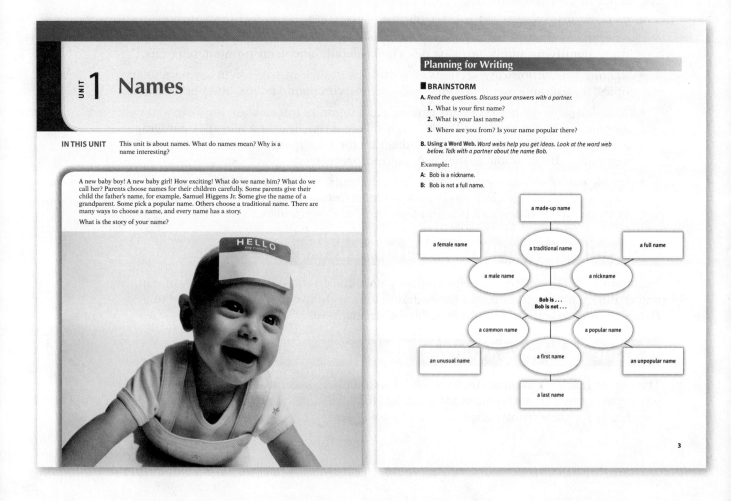

A **reading** about the topic will help you develop more ideas. The reading can be a newspaper or magazine article, a webpage, or a blog.

Building Word Knowledge activities introduce a vocabulary or dictionary skill that you will be able to use when you write your assignment. For example, you will practice using different word forms and collocations.

■READ

Read the article about rules for names.

www.babynames.com

Let's name the baby "@"

1 In the United States, there are no rules about names. Sometimes parents choose a common name, such as John. Sometimes they choose an unusual name, such as Candy Apple or Table. Often a child has the name of a family member or a famous person. Children can even have made-up names, such as Blahj or Abcde.

2 Other countries have rules about names. In China, for example, names must use Chinese characters. One Chinese couple learned this rule a few years ago. They wanted to name their child "@." "@" is not a Chinese character. It is a symbol in an email address. In China, people pronounce "@" as "ai-ta." This sounds like "love him" in Mandarin. It sounds like a good name, but the Chinese government said, "No. It is against the rules." There are two reasons for this rule: Chinese computers cannot read unusual symbols on identity cards, and Chinese speakers cannot pronounce uncommon names.

3 Sweden also has naming rules. In 1991, a Swedish couple wanted to name their child "Albin." They wanted to spell the name "Brfxxccxxmnpcccclllmmnprxvclmnckssqlbb111163" or "A." The government said no. In Sweden, a name cannot be unusual or made-up. It cannot make the child uncomfortable.

4 Other countries have rules about names too. In Denmark, parents choose a name from a list of 7,000 names: 3,000 names are for boys, and 4,000 names are for girls. Other names are usually not OK. In Germany, a parent cannot give a child the name of a product. For example, a child cannot have the name of a food, hotel, car, or restaurant.

5 Are there rules for names in your country? It's always good to know the rules. It can save time and trouble.

Names **5**

Building Word Knowledge

Word Partners. In English, certain pairs of words go together. Learn these pairs. They help you build word knowledge and write well.

Here are some common word partners. They include adjectives + the word *name.*

first name

last name

full name

Read "Let's name the baby '@'" again. Write the adjective + name pairs.

Example:

common name

1. _____ name

2. _____ name

3. _____ name

4. _____ name

Comprehension

A. *Read "Let's name the baby '@' " again. Look at the chart. Make guesses. Where are the names OK for people? Check (✓) the countries and discuss your answers with a partner.*

	United States	China	Sweden	Germany
1. Male names	✓	✓	✓	✓
2. A car name				
3. The name "A"				
4. A name with Chinese characters				
5. The name "McDonald's Restaurant"				
6. A grandmother's name				
7. An unusual name				
8. A traditional name				

6 UNIT 1

■ STEP 1: PREWRITING

This section helps you further develop your ideas. It gives you a short explanation of the writing assignment.

> The **Your Own Writing** section gives you a choice of two writing assignments. After you choose one of the assignments, you can begin to think about what you will write and share your ideas with a partner (**Checking in**). Putting your ideas into a **graphic organizer** will help you structure your ideas.

Writing Sentences

In this unit, you write sentences about names. A **sentence** is a group of words. A sentence has a subject and a verb. It begins with a capital letter and ends with a period.

Step 1   Prewriting

Prewriting is important. It helps you get ideas, and it helps you prepare to write. In this prewriting, first you choose your assignment. Then you practice writing sentences about it.

Your Own Writing

Choosing Your Assignment

A. *Choose Assignment 1 or Assignment 2.*

   Assignment 1: Write about your name or a friend's name.

   Assignment 2: Write about a name you like.

B. *Make a list of names. Then write words to describe each name. This will help you choose and describe the name for your assignment.*

Names	Descriptions
Robert	popular, male
Coco	unusual, nickname

C. Checking in. *Share your list of names with a partner. Describe the names. Ask your partner questions.*

Examples:

Where are the names from?

Are they uncommon names?

Are they traditional names?

Are they nicknames?

Do you like the names?

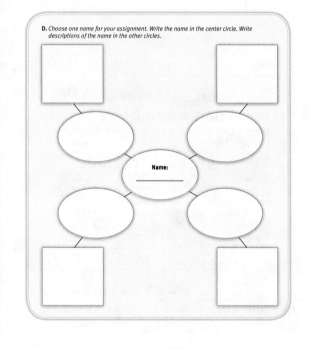

D. *Choose one name for your assignment. Write the name in the center circle. Write descriptions of the name in the other circles.*

Name: _____

STEP 2: WRITING THE FIRST DRAFT

This section guides you through each part of your writing assignment. For a paragraph assignment, you will learn how to write a topic sentence, body sentences, and concluding sentence. At the end of Step 2, you will be able to write a complete first draft.

> **Focused Practice** activities will give you lots of writing practice *before* you draft your writing assignment. Make sure to look at all of the examples and models before you complete the exercises. A useful **Tip for Writers** gives you specific writing tools, for example, how to use conjunctions to connect ideas.

Step 2   Writing the First Draft

■ SUBJECT-VERB ORDER

An English sentence has a **subject** and a **verb**. The subject comes before the verb. Sometimes the subject is a person (*Bob, he, my friends*). Sometimes the subject is a thing (*my name, it, China*). Often the verb is a form of *be*. The information after *be* describes the subject (*beautiful*). The verb can also describe an action (*pronounce, choose*) or a feeling (*like*).

Examples:

Subject	Verb	
My name	is	Bob.
Bob	is	short for Robert.
I	like	my name.

Focused Practice

A. *Read each sentence. Circle the subject. Underline the verb.*

Example:

Some people choose unusual names.

1. ꞏꞏꞏꞏꞏ
2. I like the name Morgan.
3. It is a popular name.
4. Chinese names use Chinese characters.
5. Google is an untraditional name.
6. My first name is Al.

Tip for Writers

Short Lists with *And* and *Or*. Writers often put short lists in sentences. When you make a short list, write *and* or *or* between the last two items. Put a comma between the items. Here are some examples.

*Jonathan Gold eats **grasshoppers, prawns, octopus, and jellyfish**.*

*You can have **soda, milk, apple juice, or water**.*

A. *Underline the words in each list. Add commas.*

Example:

Are tacos Mexican, Thai, Chinese, or Brazilian?

1. I don't like carrots potatoes or peas.
2. Jellyfish octopus and prawns come from the ocean.
3. Do you want chocolate mint vanilla strawberry or coffee ice cream?
4. I'm full! I ate turkey potatoes gravy sausages vegetables and chocolate cake.

B. *Complete the sentences. Use the information from the chart and write a short list in each sentence.*

Average Ranking	Restaurant	Adjectives to Describe the Food
★★★★★	Paco's Tacos	good, fun, inexpensive
★★★★	Mel's Diner	good, greasy, inexpensive
★★★★	Roma	good, friendly, expensive
★★★★	Noodle House	fun, friendly, inexpensive
★★★⚬	Chow	healthy, expensive, tasty
★★	Le Charm	fancy, expensive, OK

Example:

Paco's Tacos is *good, fun, and inexpensive.*

1. _____ are three inexpensive restaurants.
2. _____ have four stars.
3. Chow is a _____ restaurant.
4. _____ are good restaurants.
5. Le Charm is _____

STEP 3: REVISING

After you write your first draft, you aren't finished yet! Step 3 shows you how to revise your draft to make your writing better. Revising means changing sentences or words or ideas. When you revise, you try to make your writing clearer for the reader.

> Review and analyze the **model** sentences and paragraphs to get an idea of what a well-written sentence or paragraph looks like. You may see another Tip for Writers or Building Word Knowledge box to help you fit the parts of your own writing together.
>
> Completing the **Revision Checklists** for each writing assignment will help you identify parts of your draft that need improvement.

Step 3 Revising

Revising your draft makes your writing better. Revising means changing sentences, words, or ideas. When you revise, you try to make your writing clearer for your reader.

Tip for Writers

Reasons and Examples. When you write about your opinion, you need to include reasons and examples. Reasons and examples help explain your opinion. When the reasons and examples do not explain your opinion, they are not helpful to the reader. Remove irrelevant (not helpful) reasons and examples from your paragraph.

A. Read each topic sentence. Circle the two reasons or examples that explain the opinion in the topic sentence.

Example:

Topic Sentence: I think a lot of soccer posters, magazines, and sports equipment make a room comfortable.

a. For example, Pele was a really famous Brazilian soccer player, so I want to meet him.

(b.) For instance, I love reading about my favorite soccer players, so my room is full of sports magazines.

(c.) For example, I have a lot of equipment in my room because I love playing soccer.

1. **Topic Sentence:** I think my favorite books make my living room homey.
   a. I lie on the couch and read all the time.
   b. Books make me feel comfortable.
   c. My couch is an important part of my living room too.

2. **Topic Sentence:** I always carry a photo of my brother and me from 1989.
   a. My brother and I travelled together that year.
   b. The photo brings back memories of our travels.
   c. My brother is an engineer now.

3. **Topic Sentence:** Photos on a fridge always make a kitchen homey.
   a. For instance, the calendar on my refrigerator organizes my days.
   b. For example, the picture of my hometown in Guatemala makes me feel at home.
   c. For instance, the photo of my husband makes me happy.

4. Are there examples or reasons? List them.

_____

_____

5. Does the conclusion do one of the following? Check (✓) the answer.

_____ talk about the future

_____ summarize the opinion paragraph

_____ add an additional opinion

B. Work with a partner. Compare your answers.

Your Own Writing

Revising Your Draft

A. Look at your paragraph on page 141. Then read the Revision Checklist and check (✓) your answers. What do you need to revise?

B. Revise your paragraph. Remember: Cross out irrelevant reasons and examples. Add helpful reasons and examples to make your opinion clear for the reader.

Revision Checklist	Yes	No
1. Underline the topic sentence.		
Did you name an item that makes you feel at home or makes a space homey?		
2. Circle the item in your topic sentence.		
Did you say why this item is important to you?		
3. Number the reasons and examples in the body sentences.		
Do all the reasons and examples help the reader understand your opinion?		
4. Underline the conclusion.		
Does the conclusion do one of the following:		
• tell about the future?		
• summarize the paragraph?		
• add an opinion to the topic sentence?		
5. Put a star (*) next to each new word or phrase from this unit.		
Are there at least two new words or phrases?		

STEP 4: EDITING

In the final step, you review a grammar topic that will help you edit your revised draft. Then you use an Editing Checklist to correct your own paragraph for any errors in grammar, punctuation, or capitalization.

> **Grammar Presentation** charts present notes and examples on specific grammar topics related to your writing assignment. Follow up with grammar practice.
>
> **Editing Checklists** for each writing assignment help you correct and polish your final draft.

Step 4 Editing

GRAMMAR PRESENTATION

Before you hand in your sentences, look at them one more time and edit them. Look for errors in capitalization, punctuation, and grammar. In this editing section, you review the present of the verb *be*. Think about your sentences as you review.

Present of *Be*: Statements

Grammar Notes	Examples
1. The **present** of **be** has three forms: **am**, **is**, and **are**	• I **am** from Seattle. • Gus **is** my nickname. • They **are** traditional names.
2. Use the correct form of **be + not** to make a **negative statement**.	• I **am not** from Sydney. • Sam **is not** my real name. • We **are not** Italian.
3. We often use **contractions** (short forms) in speaking and informal writing. **Note:** There are two negative contractions for **is not** and **are not**. We often use **isn't** or **aren't** after subject nouns. We often use **'s not** or **'re not** after subject pronouns.	• I'**m** June. I'**m not** Jane. • **John isn't** my first name. **It's not** my nickname. **It's** my family name. • **Mae and Jean aren't** my first names. **They're not** my last names. **They're** my middle names.

Focused Practice

A. *Read the sentences. Circle the forms of the verb be in each sentence.*

Example:
Amy (is) an Australian name.

1. She isn't from Australia.
2. They aren't from my country.
3. Our names are famous artists' names.
4. My name is a common French name.

B. *Complete the sentences with the correct form of the verb be.*

Example:
José and Javier _____are_____ Mexican.

1. Vladimir and I _____ Ukranian.
2. I _____ a Canadian.
3. You and Lisbet _____ from Denmark.
4. The name Joe _____ not unusual.

C. *Correct the use of the verb be in the sentences. Add the verb when needed.*

Example:
Gabriel are a male name.
Gabriel is a male name.

1. They Brazilian names.

_____

2. The nickname for Gabriel are Gabe.

_____

3. My name am not unusual.

_____

4. I is called Joe for short.

_____

5. We from Canada.

Your Own Writing

Editing Your Draft

A. *Edit your sentences for the assignment. Use the Editing Checklist below.*

B. *Write a clean copy of your sentences. Give it to your teacher.*

Editing Checklist		
Did you . . .	**Yes**	**No**
• use the present of the verb *be* correctly?		
• use vocabulary from the unit correctly?		
• use capital letters and periods?		
• use complete sentences?		
• describe a name clearly?		

Now, you are ready to begin with Unit 1. Enjoy the writing process!

Scope and Sequence

UNIT	STEP 1 Planning and Prewriting	STEP 2 Writing the First Draft

1 Names
 	
Writing Focus
Writing simple sentences
 	
Reading
Let's name the baby "@",
about rules for names
	Using a word web
	Using word partners: adjective +
	   name
	Capitalizing names
	Making a list of names and
	   descriptions
	Choosing a writing assignment for
	   sentences about names
	Sharing ideas and creating a word
	   web for the assignment
		Writing simple sentences
		Identifying subject and verb
		Putting subject and verb in order
		Finding information online about
		   unusual names

2 Do-It-Yourself
 	
Writing Focus
Writing simple sentences
 	
Reading
The Maker Faire,
about a DIY fair
	Using a process chart
	Using reflexive pronouns
	Using ordinal numbers
	Making a list of do-it-yourself projects
	Choosing a writing assignment for
	   sentences about a do-it-yourself
	   project
	Sharing ideas and creating a process
	   chart for the assignment
	Building dictionary skills through
	   word families
		Writing simple sentences
		Identifying the subject of a sentence
		Identifying imperative statements
		Finding information online about
		   do-it-yourself projects

3 Food
 	
Writing Focus
Writing a basic paragraph
 	
Reading
The Restaurant Critic,
about Jonathan Gold, Los
Angeles restaurant critic
	Using a ranking chart
	Using opposites: *adjectives*
	Using short lists with *and* and *or*
	Making a list and describing food
	   and dishes
	Choosing a writing assignment for a
	   paragraph about food
	Sharing ideas and creating a ranking
	   chart for the assignment
		Writing the topic
		Using the suffix *-ed* to form adjectives
		Using correct parts of speech in
		   short lists
		Finding information online about food
		Writing simple sentences about food

STEP 3 Revising	STEP 4 Editing	Learning Outcome	*Focus on Grammar Level 1, Third Edition*
Using words about names: *nickname, initials* Capitalizing and punctuating simple sentences Analyzing model sentences Applying the Revision Checklist and writing the second draft	Reviewing the present of *be* in statements Incorporating the grammar in sentences Applying the Editing Checklist and writing the final draft	Can write simple phrases and sentences about yourself or someone you know.	**Unit 3** Present of *Be*: Statements
Using word categories Using time order words Analyzing model sentences Applying the Revision Checklist and writing the second draft	Reviewing simple present statements Incorporating the grammar in sentences Applying the Editing Checklist and writing the final draft	Can write simple sentences on a topic of personal interest.	**Unit 9** Imperatives **Unit 10** Simple Present: Statements **Unit 27** *There is / There are*
Formatting a paragraph Using the prefix *un-* Writing a paragraph about food Using capitalization and end punctuation Using descriptive adjectives Analyzing a model paragraph Applying the Revision Checklist and writing the second draft	Reviewing adjective and noun modifiers Incorporating the grammar in sentences Applying the Editing Checklist and writing the final draft	Can connect sentences in a short paragraph about a familiar topic, and explain preferences.	**Unit 28** Noun and Adjective Modifiers

UNIT	STEP 1 Planning and Prewriting	STEP 2 Writing the First Draft
4 Clothes *Writing Focus* Writing a basic paragraph *Reading* *Baseball Caps for Everyone*, about a fashion statement	Using a cluster chart Using synonyms Using word categories; ordering words Making a list of favorite and practical clothes Choosing a writing assignment for a paragraph about clothes Sharing ideas and creating a cluster chart for the assignment	Writing the topic sentence and controlling idea Writing paragraph titles Finding information online about clothes Writing a paragraph about clothes
5 Amazing Nature *Writing Focus* Writing a basic paragraph *Reading* *The Storm Chaser*, about Warren Faidley, a famous photographer	Using a *wh-* questions chart Using word partners: noun + *storm* Using time order words: *before, during, after* Creating a vocabulary log Making a list of natural events Choosing a writing assignment for a paragraph about natural events Sharing ideas and creating a *wh-* questions chart for the assignment	Writing the topic sentence and controlling idea Writing body sentences Using sense verbs Finding information online about natural events Writing a paragraph about a natural event
6 Helping Hands *Writing Focus* Writing a basic paragraph *Reading* *The Thorn Tree Project*, about a volunteer project in Kenya	Using a main idea / supporting details chart Using word families with *help* Brainstorming for the assignment Choosing a writing assignment for a paragraph about helping others Sharing ideas and creating a main idea / supporting details chart for the assignment	Writing the topic sentence and controlling idea Writing body sentences Writing the concluding sentence Finding information online about helping Expressing reasons with *because* Writing a paragraph about helping

STEP 3 Revising	STEP 4 Editing	Learning Outcome	*Focus on Grammar Level 1, Third Edition*
Using expressions with *keep* Applying rules for writing titles Analyzing a model paragraph Applying the Revision Checklist and writing the second draft	Reviewing *a*, *an*, and *the* Incorporating the grammar in sentences Applying the Editing Checklist and writing the final draft	Can connect ideas in a paragraph expressing personal feelings and describing clothing.	**Unit 20** *A / An* and *The*
Using Antonyms Connecting ideas with *and, but,* and *so* Analyzing a model paragraph Applying the Revision Checklist and writing the second draft	Reviewing the simple past of regular and irregular verbs Incorporating the grammar in sentences Applying the Editing Checklist and writing the final draft	Can write a short paragraph describing an amazing experience in the past and impressions of the experience.	**Unit 7** Past of *Be*: Statements; *Yes / No* Questions **Unit 5** Simple Past: Regular and Irregular Verbs; *Yes / No* Questions
Using the suffix *-ful* Answering *how* questions with *by* + verb + *-ing* Analyzing a model paragraph Applying the Revision Checklist and writing the second draft	Reviewing subject and object pronouns Incorporating the grammar in sentences Applying the Editing Checklist and writing the final draft	Can write a short, clear paragraph describing an important experience.	**Unit 25** Subject and Object Pronouns

UNIT	STEP 1 Planning and Prewriting	STEP 2 Writing the First Draft
7 Home Sweet Home *Writing Focus* Writing an opinion paragraph *Reading* *New Houses for the Lower Ninth Ward*, about a neighborhood in New Orleans	Using an E-chart Using expressions with *home* Using expressions with *make + someone / something* + adjective Brainstorming for the assignment Choosing a writing assignment for an opinion paragraph Sharing ideas and creating an E-chart for the assignment	Writing a topic sentence that states an opinion Writing body sentences that give reasons and examples to support an opinion Writing a concluding sentence that adds a final opinion, summarizes the paragraph, or talks about the future Finding information online about "feeling at home" Introducing examples with *for instance, for example* Writing an opinion paragraph
8 Luck *Writing Focus* Writing a narrative paragraph *Reading* *The Flight of the Gossamer Albatross*, about a lucky situation	Using a timeline Using word families with *luck* Using time expressions to order events Brainstorming for the assignment Choosing a writing assignment for a narrative paragraph Sharing ideas and creating a timeline for the assignment	Writing a topic sentence that introduces the story Writing body sentences that tell the story Writing a concluding sentence that comments on the story Finding information online about lucky people and situations Using descriptive language Writing a narrative paragraph

STEP 3 Revising	STEP 4 Editing	Learning Outcome	*Focus on Grammar Level 1, Third Edition*
Supporting opinions with relevant reasons and examples Analyzing a model opinion paragraph Applying the Revision Checklist and writing the second draft	Reviewing count and non-count nouns Incorporating the grammar in sentences Applying the Editing Checklist and writing the final draft	Can write a short, clear paragraph that supports and gives reasons for an opinion.	**Unit 19** Count and Non-count Nouns
Avoiding sentence fragments Using expressions about luck Analyzing a model narrative paragraph Applying the Revision Checklist and writing the second draft	Reviewing the prepositions *in, on, at* + time Incorporating the grammar in sentences Applying the Editing Checklist and writing the final draft	Can write a short, clear paragraph that tells a story about a lucky event.	**Unit 20** Prepositions of Time: *in, on, at*

UNIT 1 Names

IN THIS UNIT This unit is about names. What do names mean? Why is a name interesting?

A new baby boy! A new baby girl! How exciting! What do we name him? What do we call her? Parents choose names for their children carefully. Some parents give their child the father's name, for example, Samuel Higgens Jr. Some give the name of a grandparent. Some pick a popular name. Others choose a traditional name. There are many ways to choose a name, and every name has a story.

What is the story of your name?

Planning for Writing

■BRAINSTORM

A. *Read the questions. Discuss your answers with a partner.*

1. What is your first name?

2. What is your last name?

3. Where are you from? Is your name popular there?

B. Using a Word Web. *Word webs help you get ideas. Look at the word web below. Talk with a partner about the name Bob.*

Example:

A: Bob is a nickname.

B: Bob is not a full name.

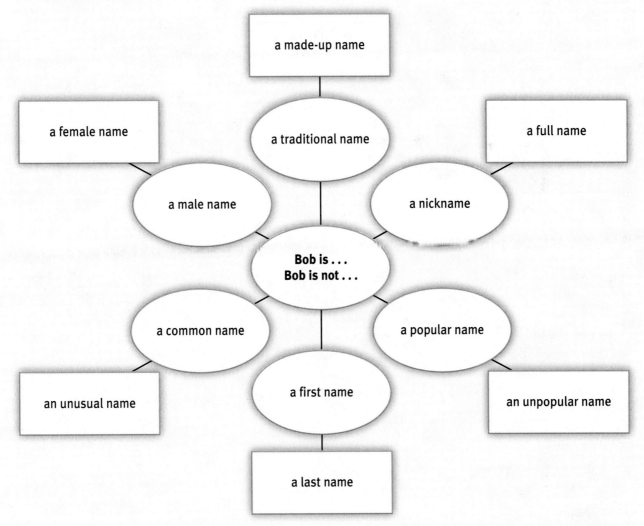

C. *Write your name in the center of the word web below. Complete the web. Use words from Exercise B.*

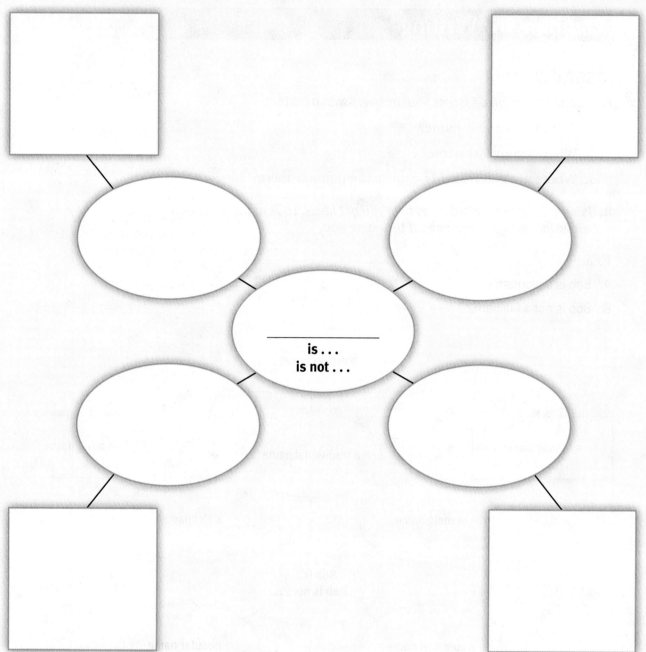

_____

is . . .
is not . . .

Read the article about rules for names.

www.babynames.com

Let's name the baby "@"

1 In the United States, there are no rules about names. Sometimes parents choose a common name, such as John. Sometimes they choose an unusual name, such as Candy Apple or Table. Often a child has the name of a family member or a famous person. Children can even have made-up names, such as Blahj or Abcde.

2 Other countries have rules about names. In China, for example, names must use Chinese characters. One Chinese couple learned this rule a few years ago. They wanted to name their child "@." "@" is not a Chinese character. It is a symbol in an email address. In China, people pronounce "@" as "ai-ta." This sounds like "love him" in Mandarin. It sounds like a good name, but the Chinese government said, "No. It is against the rules." There are two reasons for this rule: Chinese computers cannot read unusual symbols on identity cards, and Chinese speakers cannot pronounce uncommon names.

3 Sweden also has naming rules. In 1991, a Swedish couple wanted to name their child "Albin." They wanted to spell the name "Brfxxccxxmnpcccclllmmnprxvclmnckssqlbb111163" or "A." The government said no. In Sweden, a name cannot be unusual or made-up. It cannot make the child uncomfortable.

4 Other countries have rules about names too. In Denmark, parents choose a name from a list of 7,000 names: 3,000 names are for boys, and 4,000 names are for girls. Other names are usually not OK. In Germany, a parent cannot give a child the name of a product. For example, a child cannot have the name of a food, hotel, car, or restaurant.

5 Are there rules for names in your country? It's always good to know the rules. It can save time and trouble.

Building Word Knowledge

Word Partners. In English, certain pairs of words go together. Learn these pairs. They help you build word knowledge and write well.

Here are some common word partners. They include adjectives + the word *name*.

first name

last name

full name

Read "Let's name the baby '@' " again. Write the adjective + name *pairs.*

Example:

common name

1. _____ name

2. _____ name

3. _____ name

4. _____ name

Comprehension

A. *Read "Let's name the baby '@' " again. Look at the chart. Make guesses. Where are the names OK for people? Check (✓) the countries and discuss your answers with a partner.*

	United States	China	Sweden	Germany
1. Male names	✓	✓	✓	✓
2. A car name				
3. The name "A"				
4. A name with Chinese characters				
5. The name "McDonald's Restaurant"				
6. A grandmother's name				
7. An unusual name				
8. A traditional name				

B. *Complete the word web about the name "@".*

Hi, my name is @.

What kind of name is @?

a common name

"@" is not . . .

C. *Think about the reading. Read the questions and discuss your answers with a partner.*

1. I live in Germany. Is it OK to name my baby "1A"?

2. Is it OK to name my baby "@" in Denmark and Sweden?

3. In the United States, there is a song called "A Boy Named Sue." "Sue" is usually a female name. Is it OK to name a boy "Sue"?

4. Parents want to call their daughter "Google." Is that OK in the United States?

5. Do you have a traditional name? Do you think you can give a child your name in other countries?

Tip for Writers

Capitalizing Names. People's names begin with a capital letter.

A. *Circle the capital letters in the row below.*

a b c Ⓓ E f G h I j K l m n O P Q R s T u v W X y Z

B. *Write the names of two classmates. Remember to capitalize the first letter of each name.*

Example:

Shu Bing Zhang

1. _____   2. _____

Writing Sentences

In this unit, you write sentences about names. A **sentence** is a group of words. A sentence has a subject and a verb. It begins with a capital letter and ends with a period.

Step 1   Prewriting

Prewriting is important. It helps you get ideas, and it helps you prepare to write. In this prewriting, first you choose your assignment. Then you practice writing sentences about it.

Your Own Writing

Choosing Your Assignment

A. *Choose Assignment 1 or Assignment 2.*

> **Assignment 1:** Write about your name or a friend's name.
>
> **Assignment 2:** Write about a name you like.

B. *Make a list of names. Then write words to describe each name. This will help you choose and describe the name for your assignment.*

Names	Descriptions
Robert	popular, male
Coco	unusual, nickname

C. Checking in. *Share your list of names with a partner. Describe the names. Ask your partner questions.*

Examples:

Where are the names from?

Are they uncommon names?

Are they traditional names?

Are they nicknames?

Do you like the names?

D. *Choose one name for your assignment. Write the name in the center circle. Write descriptions of the name in the other circles.*

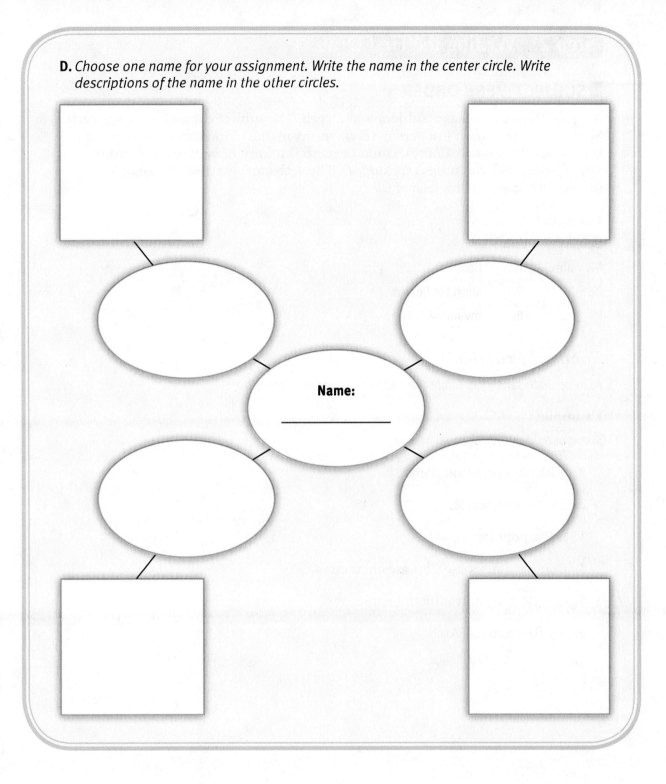

■ SUBJECT-VERB ORDER

An English sentence has a **subject** and a **verb**. The subject comes before the verb. Sometimes the subject is a person (*Bob, he, my friends*). Sometimes the subject is a thing (*my name, it, China*). Often the verb is a form of *be*. The information after *be* describes the subject (*beautiful*). The verb can also describe an action (*pronounce, choose*) or a feeling (*like*).

Examples:

Subject	Verb	
My name	is	Bob.
Bob	is	short for Robert.
I	like	my name.

Focused Practice

A. *Read each sentence. Circle the subject. Underline the verb.*

Example:

(Some people) choose unusual names.

1. Yoshi is a common name.

2. I like the name Morgan.

3. It is a popular name.

4. Chinese names use Chinese characters.

5. Google is an untraditional name.

6. My first name is Al.

B. *Make sentences. Write the words in the correct order.*

Example:

Surasawadee / my first name / is

Surasawadee is my first name.

1. is / a Thai name / It

_____

2. "Surasawadee" / knowledge / means

_____

3. My friends / Dee / call me

_____

4. short and easy / is / The name Dee

_____

5. like / I / my name

_____

C. *Correct the sentences. Add a subject or a verb.*

Example:

Her name Yung Cho.

Her name is Yung Cho.

1. Joe my nickname.

_____

2. My name a made-up name.

_____

3. Sounds like "love him."

_____

4. It a Chinese name is.

_____

5. My name popular.

_____

Your Own Writing

Finding Out More

A. *Go online. Type the keywords* unusual names *or* names from [your country]. *Find information about the name for your assignment. Find information about other names you like. Find information about your own name too.*

B. *Write the names in the chart. Answer the questions.*

	Name _____	**Name** _____	**Name** _____
Where is the name from?			
Is it a popular name?			
What is the meaning of the name?			
Is it a male or a female name?			
Is it a traditional name or an unusual name?			
Other information:			

C. Checking in. *Share your information about names with a partner. Add names you like from your partner's list.*

Planning Your Sentences

A. *Look at the names in your chart. Choose the name for your assignment. You can choose the name in your word web on page 9, or you can choose a name from Exercise B above.*

B. Writing for the Assignment. *Write three or more sentences about the name.*

Example:

I like the name Allen.

Allen is a boy's name.

It is a common name in the United States.

_____

_____

_____

_____

_____

Revising your draft is another important step. Revising means you make changes to your writing. For example, you add new words or new information. Revising makes your writing better.

Building Word Knowledge

Words about Names. In the United States, people usually use first names to talk to friends. Sometimes people do not use their real first name. They use another name. Here are some examples.

Real Name	Other Name
Given name: James Robert	*Initials:* JR
Given name: Kevin	*Short for* Kevin: Kev
Given name: Jennifer	*Nickname:* Sport

A. *Look at the picture and read the conversations out loud with a partner.*

B. *Work with a partner. Match the words and the meanings.*

1. call someone   _____ **a.** last name

2 it's short for . . .   _____ **b.** name that is not the real name; often it describes a person's personality

3. initial

4. middle name   _____ **c.** name between your first and last names

     _____ **d.** first letter of a name

5. nickname

     _____ **e.** name on the birth certificate; official name

6. family name

     _____ **f.** abbreviated name; not a full, long name

7. given name

     _1_ **g.** give someone a name

C. *Some students filled out information cards for their teacher. Read each one. Explain the name. Write one or two sentences.*

Example:

D. *Write about the name for your assignment. Check (✓) the answer.*

| Name: Genevieve Linda Miller |
| first   middle   last |
| What do you want me to call you? |
| Jenny |

Call her _Jenny_ .

Jenny is short for Genevieve.

1.

| Name: John   Paul   Collins |
| first   middle   last |
| What do you want me to call you? |
| JP |

Call him _____ .

_____

2.

| Name: Mary   Rose   Emley |
| first   middle   last |
| What do you want me to call you? |
| Rose |

Call her _____ .

_____

3.

| Name: Hyun   Rae   Park |
| first   middle   last |
| What do you want me to call you? |
| Elvis |

Call him _____ .

_____

1. Is it short for a name? _____ yes _____ no

What is the full name? _____

2. Is there a common nickname for this name? _____ yes _____ no

What is the nickname? _____

3. Is it usually a given name? _____ yes _____ no

Is it usually a middle name? _____ yes _____ no

Is it usually a family name? _____ yes _____ no

Tip for Writers

Capitalization and Punctuation. Remember that simple sentences always begin with a capital letter and end with a period. Use capital letters to begin proper nouns too. Proper nouns are the names of places (Sweden), languages (Swedish), people (Maria), and titles (*Toy Story*).

Correct the sentences. Use capital letters and periods.

Example:

my father's name is fred

My father's name is Fred.

1. fred is a popular name in our family

_____

2. my grandfather's name is fred too

_____

3. fred is short for frederick

_____

4. it is a german name

_____

5. my grandfather comes from germany

_____

6. my father's real name is not common in our family

_____

Focused Practice

A. *Read the sentences and answer the questions.*

> My first name is Natasha.
>
> It means Christmas.
>
> It is Russian, but I am not Russian.
>
> Natasha is a traditional name in Russia.
>
> It is an untraditional name in the United States.
>
> My name is a girl's name in the movie *War and Peace*.
>
> My sister calls me Tash for short.
>
> I like my real name and my nickname.

1. What name are the sentences about? Circle the name.

2. Count the sentences. How many sentences are there? _____

3. Do the sentences answer at least two of these questions? Check (✓) the questions.

   ☐ What does the name mean?

   ☐ What country is it from?

   ☐ Is it a traditional name?

   ☐ What is the name short for?

   ☐ Does it have a nickname?

4. Underline the new vocabulary words from this unit. How many are there? _____

5. Circle the capital letters in each sentence. Circle the period at the end of each sentence.

B. *Work with a partner. Compare your answers.*

Your Own Writing

Revising Your Draft

A. *Look at your sentences on page 12, Writing for the Assignment. Then read the Revision Checklist and check (✓) your answers. What do you need to revise?*

B. *Revise your sentences. Remember: Add capital letters and periods when needed.*

Revision Checklist	Yes	No
1. Circle the name in your sentences. Are all the sentences about the name?		
2. Count the sentences. Are there three or more sentences?		
3. Do your sentences answer at least two of these questions?		
• What does the name mean?		
• What country is it from?		
• Is it a traditional name?		
• What is the name short for?		
• Does the name have a nickname?		
4. Underline the new vocabulary words and phrases from this unit. Are there at least four new words from this unit?		
5. Circle the capital letters in the sentences. Circle the period at the end of each sentence. Are the sentences correct?		

Step 4   Editing

■ GRAMMAR PRESENTATION

Before you hand in your sentences, look at them one more time and edit them. Look for errors in capitalization, punctuation, and grammar. In this editing section, you review the present of the verb *be*. Think about your sentences as you review.

Present of *Be*: Statements

Grammar Notes	Examples
1. The **present** of *be* has three forms: *am*, *is*, and *are*	• I **am** from Seattle. • Gus **is** my nickname. • They **are** traditional names.
2. Use the correct form of *be* + *not* to make a **negative statement**.	• I **am not** from Sydney. • Sam **is not** my real name. • We **are not** Italian.
3. We often use **contractions** (short forms) in speaking and informal writing. **NOTE:** There are two negative contractions for *is not* and *are not*. We often use *isn't* or *aren't* after subject nouns. We often use *'s not* or *'re not* after subject pronouns.	• **I'm** June. **I'm not** Jane. • **John isn't** my first name. **It's not** my nickname. **It's** my family name. • **Mae and Jean aren't** my first names. **They're not** my last names. **They're** my middle names.

Focused Practice

A. *Read the sentences. Circle the forms of the verb* be *in each sentence.*

Example:

Amy (is) an Australian name.

1. She isn't from Australia.

2. They aren't from my country.

3. Our names are famous artists' names.

4. My name is a common French name.

B. *Complete the sentences with the correct form of the verb* be.

Example:

José and Javier _____*are*_____ Mexican.

1. Vladimir and I _____ Ukranian.

2. I _____ a Canadian.

3. You and Lisbet _____ from Denmark.

4. The name Joe _____ not unusual.

C. *Correct the use of the verb* be *in the sentences. Add the verb when needed.*

Example:

Gabriel are a male name.

Gabriel is a male name.

1. They Brazilian names.

   _____

2. The nickname for Gabriel are Gabe.

   _____

3. My name am not unusual.

   _____

4. I is called Joe for short.

   _____

5. We from Canada.

   _____

Your Own Writing

Editing Your Draft

A. *Edit your sentences for the assignment. Use the Editing Checklist below.*

B. *Write a clean copy of your sentences. Give it to your teacher.*

Editing Checklist		
Did you . . .	**Yes**	**No**
• use the present of the verb *be* correctly?		
• use vocabulary from the unit correctly?		
• use capital letters and periods?		
• use complete sentences?		
• describe a name clearly?		

Do-It-Yourself

IN THIS UNIT This unit is about DIY. DIY is short for "do-it-yourself." What does "do-it-yourself" mean? What are some examples of DIY projects?

In the old days, people did things themselves because it was necessary. For example, they did not go to grocery store; they grew vegetables in their own gardens. They did not go to department stores; they made their own clothes. Today, DIYers make things themselves. Many DIY projects can save money. DIY projects are fun. DIYers are always proud to say, "I made it myself."

Are you a DIYer? Do you make things yourself?

Planning for Writing

■ BRAINSTORM

A. *Read the questions. Discuss your answers with a partner.*

1. Do you like making and doing things yourself?

2. What do you make yourself?

3. What "ready-made" things do you buy at a store?

B. *Read the recipe for making mint tea. Put the recipe steps in order. Discuss your recipe with a partner. Are your recipes the same?*

Beverages

Recipe for <u>Mint tea from scratch[1]</u>

____ Add two teaspoons of sugar.[2]

__1__ Pick fresh mint.

____ Boil water[3] in a kettle.

____ Pour the tea into a tea cup[4] and enjoy!

____ Put the mint leaves[5] in a teapot.[6]

____ Wait 5 minutes.[7]

____ Wash the mint leaves carefully.

____ Pour boiling water into the teapot.

[1] **make things from scratch:** make or build things from beginning to end

[2] **teaspoon of sugar**

[3] **boil water**

[4] **teacup**

[5] **mint leaves**

[6] **teapot**

[7] **5 minutes**

C. Using a Process Chart. *Process charts help you organize steps in a process. Look at the process chart below. Complete the chart for making mint tea from scratch.*

Making Mint Tea from Scratch

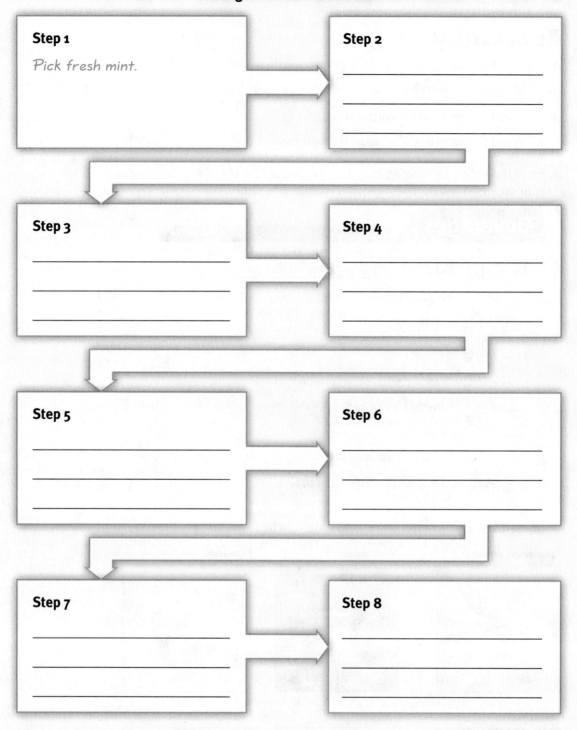

Step 1

Pick fresh mint.

Step 2

_____

_____

_____

Step 3

_____

_____

_____

Step 4

_____

_____

_____

Step 5

_____

_____

_____

Step 6

_____

_____

_____

Step 7

_____

_____

_____

Step 8

_____

_____

_____

The Maker Faire

1   The Maker Faire[1] is a big DIY festival. It takes place once a year in many U.S. cities. Old and young inventors and artists show their projects at the Maker Faire. Visitors come to see the projects and to learn how to make things themselves.

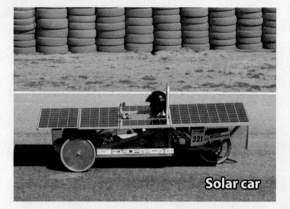

Solar car

Cupcake cars

2   Some projects are just for fun, like the electric cupcake cars. Inventors make these cars themselves. You cannot drive very far in them, but people smile at them. People also smile at the unicycle[2] with two seats. It is very difficult to ride.

3   Most projects are serious. For example, one group of people built a museum about space travel. The museum looks like a rocket. Visitors go inside and learn about space travel. There are several serious car projects at the Maker Faire too. Some cars use solar (sun) power, and some use regular electricity.

4   It's fun to see all the interesting projects at the Maker Faire, but visitors also learn things there. You can learn how to build a guitar or a table, for example. There are knitting lessons and cooking lessons. The "fix-it" workshops are very popular. You learn how to repair things yourself, like toasters and cameras.

5   After the Maker Faire, the inventors return to their workshops. Excited visitors go home and dream about the next Maker Faire. They want to come back the following year and show their own projects.

___

[1] **faire:** fair or festival
[2] **unicycle:** like a bicycle with only one wheel

Building Word Knowledge

Reflexive Pronouns. Look at the expression *do-it-yourself*. *Yourself* is a reflexive pronoun. Reflexive pronouns refer to the subject. Here is a list of reflexive pronouns. They can help you talk about DIY projects.

I do it **myself**.	*We* make it **ourselves**.
You do it **yourself**.	*You* do it **yourselves**.
He makes it **himself**.	*They* make it **themselves**.
She makes it **herself**.	

A. Read "The Maker Faire" again. Write the reflexive pronouns from the reading.

1. _____   2. _____   3. _____

B. Complete the sentences. Use the reflexive pronouns in the box.

herself	myself	ourselves	themselves	yourself

1. We do it _____.

2. They make these sweaters _____.

3. I made these cookies _____.

4. She builds houses _____.

5. You have a lot of do-it-_____ projects.

Comprehension

A. Read "The Maker Faire" again. Complete the sentences. Circle the letter of the best answer.

1. At the Maker Faire, visitors can see many _____.

   a. serious and just-for-fun DIY projects

   b. young and interesting people

   c. old cupcakes and cars

2. At the Maker Faire, visitors can learn to _____.

   a. drive different cars

   b. fix things themselves

   c. play musical instruments

3. Many Maker Faire visitors want to _____.

   a. buy projects from artists

   b. become fix-it teachers

   c. show their projects next year

B. *Write examples of just-for-fun DIY projects, serious DIY projects, and things visitors can learn at the Maker Faire.*

Just-for-Fun DIY Projects	Serious DIY Projects	Things Visitors Can Learn
1. *cupcake cars*	1.	1.
2.	2.	2.

C. *Think about the reading. Read the questions and discuss your answers with a partner.*

1. Look at the brochure of Maker Faire workshops. Then read the list of workshops. What can you learn at each workshop? Complete the chart.

http://makerfaire.com

SIGN UP FOR OUR NEWSLETTER

The Maker Faire

How-To Activities

Here are a few of the things you can learn at the Maker Faire!
• make a birdhouse
• build an electric car
• make cupcakes from scratch
• repair a watch
• make yogurt
• build your own shelves
• build a bicycle with two seats
• fix a sewing machine
• make a winter coat

Fix-It-Yourself Workship	Sewing Workshop	In-the-Kitchen Workshop	Make-It-Yourself Workshop	Car and Bike Workshop
			make a birdhouse	*build an electric car*

2. Imagine you are at the Maker Faire. Which workshops do you want to attend?

Tip for Writers

Ordinal Numbers. *First, second,* and *third* are examples of ordinal numbers. Use ordinal numbers in your writing about a process. They order the steps for the reader.

A. *Circle the ordinal numbers.*

(first)　two　three　fourth　five　sixth　seven　eighth　ninth　ten

B. *Look at the process chart for making a Secret Book Box. Write the steps using ordinal numbers.*

Making a Secret Book Box

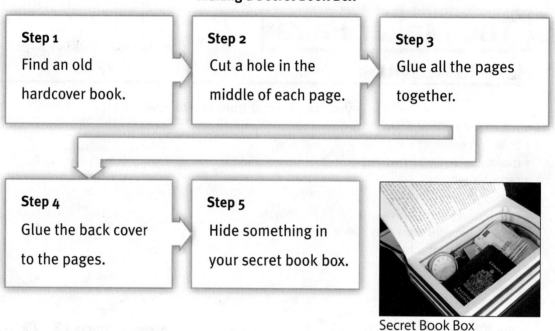

Step 1

Find an old hardcover book.

Step 2

Cut a hole in the middle of each page.

Step 3

Glue all the pages together.

Step 4

Glue the back cover to the pages.

Step 5

Hide something in your secret book box.

Secret Book Box

First, you find an old hardcover book.

_____

_____

_____

_____

Writing Sentences

In this unit, you write sentences about steps in a **process**. Sentences about a process often include time-order words. These words order the steps in the process. Remember: A sentence begins with a capital letter and ends with a period. A sentence has a subject and a verb.

Step 1   Prewriting

Prewriting is important. It helps you get ideas, and it helps you prepare to write. In this prewriting, first you choose your assignment. Then you practice writing sentences about the steps in a process.

Your Own Writing

Choosing Your Assignment

A. *Choose Assignment 1 or Assignment 2.*

> **Assignment 1:** Write about a fun do-it-yourself project, for example, making a new dessert.

> **Assignment 2:** Write about a serious do-it-yourself project, for example, building a bookcase.

B. *Read the list of do-it-yourself projects. Check (✓) the projects you like. This will help you choose a project for your assignment.*

_____ sew kitchen curtains   _____ paint your room

_____ take a picture   _____ build a website

_____ knit a sweater   _____ make homemade cleaning products

_____ bake a cake   _____ build a model airplane

_____ grow tomatoes   _____ make an ugly bike

_____ fix a light   _____ your own ideas: _____

_____ build a tree house   _____

C. Checking in. *Share your list of projects with a partner. Ask your partner questions. Add projects you like to your list.*

Examples:

What projects do you like?

Do you do the projects yourself?

What are some steps for the projects?

D. *Choose one project for your assignment. Write the name of the project. Then write the steps for the project in the process chart.*

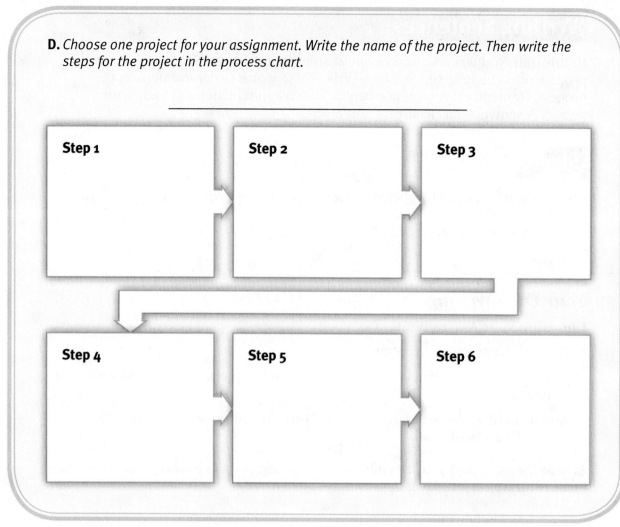

Building Word Knowledge

Dictionary Skills: Word Families. A dictionary helps you understand the meaning of words. It also helps you use the words correctly. Sometimes the same word is different parts of speech, for example, a noun and a verb. Sometimes the same word has several meanings. A dictionary helps you choose the right meaning.

Here are some words to describe steps in DIY projects. These words describe putting things together. A dictionary helps you use these words correctly in your writing.

attach	sew	tape
glue	staple	tie
nail		

A. *Use a dictionary. Write the meaning(s) of the words. Write the best meanings for a do-it-yourself project.*

Example:

glue

(*noun*) a sticky substance used for attaching things together

(*verb*) to join things together using glue

1. nail

   (*noun*) _____

   (*verb*) _____

2. tape

   (*noun*) _____

   (*verb*) _____

3. sew

   (*verb*) _____

4. tie

   (*noun*) _____

   (*verb*) _____

5. staple

   (*noun*) _____

   (*verb*) _____

6. attach

   (*verb*) _____

B. *Check (✓) the best answers.*

What do people usually . . .	Paper	Wood	Cloth	String
1. nail together?		✓		
2. glue together?				
3. tape together?				
4. sew together?				
5. staple together?				
6. tie together?				

■ SUBJECT OF A SIMPLE SENTENCE

An English sentence has a **subject** and a verb. The subject comes before the verb. In most sentences the subject is a person or a thing. Sometimes the subject is ***there***.

In **imperative** sentences, the subject is ***you***. In imperative sentences, you do not need to write *you*.

Grammar Notes	Examples
1. Sentences have a **subject** and a <u>verb</u>. The subject is a **noun** or a **pronoun**.	• The **Maker Faire** <u>is</u> a DIY fair. • **Artists** <u>show</u> their projects at the fair. • **They** <u>want</u> to come back next year.
2. Use ***there is*** or ***there's*** to state facts about a person or thing. **Use *there are*** if the noun is plural. **Be Careful!** Don't use a plural noun after ***there's***.	• **There is** a rocket at the Maker Faire. • **There are** several serious car projects. Not: ~~There's~~ knitting lessons and cooking lessons.
3. Use the **imperative** for instructions. **Use** the **base form** of the verb for the imperative. **Use *do not*** or ***don't*** + the **base form** for the **negative** form of the imperative.	• **Do** it yourself. • **Don't buy** it at a store.

Focused Practice

A. *Read the sentences. Circle the subject. Underline the verb.*

Example:

(My dad) makes very tall bikes.

1. He makes them himself.

2. He calls them double bikes.

3. He attaches two bicycles together.

4. There is one seat on top.

5. It is very high.

6. Double bikes are dangerous.

B. *Read the sentences. Check (✓) the imperative sentences.*

_____ **1.** Don't go to the store yourselves.

_____ **2.** First, she puts the tea in the teapot.

_____ **3.** Nail the pieces of wood together.

_____ **4.** They glue the paper on the cardboard.

_____ **5.** We want to make several Secret Book Boxes.

_____ **6.** Fix the bicycle yourself.

_____ **7.** Mix the eggs and milk together.

_____ **8.** There are fix-it workshops and interesting projects.

C. *Correct the sentences. Correct the subject or verb.*

1. There are a do-it-yourself instruction book.

_____

2. Is a very easy project

_____

3. Not use a lot of sugar.

_____

4. Like arts and crafts.

_____

5. I a DIYer.

_____

6. There is lots of interesting things at the Maker Faire.

_____

Your Own Writing

Finding Out More

A. *Go online. Type the keywords* [the name of your project] *or* do-it-yourself. *Find information about the do-it-yourself project for your assignment. Find information about another interesting project too.*

B. *Write the project names in the chart. Answer the questions.*

	Project Name _____	Project Name _____
Is this a serious project or a just-for-fun project?		
How many steps are there?		
What is the first step?		
What is the second step?		
What is the third step?		
Are there other steps?		
Other information:		

C. Checking in. *Share your information about the projects with a partner. Add projects you like from your partner's list.*

Planning Your Sentences

A. *Look at the projects in your chart. Choose the project for your assignment. You can choose the project in your Process Chart on page 28, or you can choose a project from Exercise B above.*

B. Writing for the Assignment. *Write five or more sentences about the project.*

Example:

I like crossword puzzles.

I write puzzles myself.

First, I write the words.

Second, I write the clues.

Third, I draw the boxes.

_____

_____

_____

_____

_____

Step 3　Revising

Revising your draft is another important step. Revising makes your writing better. You revise when you have new information or ideas. Using a checklist, such as the Revision Checklist on page 35, can help you revise your writing.

Building Word Knowledge

Word Categories. For do-it-yourself projects, you need tools and supplies. Here are a few examples. Use your dictionary. It helps you understand the words.

To sew

tools: *needle, sewing machine*

supplies: *thread, button*

To knit

tools: *needle, tape measure*

supplies: *yarn, pattern*

To nail

tools: *hammer, tape measure*

supplies: *wood, nails*

To cut

tools: *pair of scissors, saw*

supplies: *paper, wood*

To cook

tools: *bowl, spoon, pan*

supplies: *eggs, milk*

To measure

tools: *measuring cup, spoon, ruler, tape measure*

supplies: *milk, salt, yarn*

A. *Complete the steps. Use words from the Building Word Knowledge box.*

1.

To cook scrambled eggs

Mix two eggs with milk in a _____.

Pour the eggs in a _____ and cook for 1 minute.

Stir with a _____ until cooked. Then serve.

2.

To knit a simple scarf

Find some interesting _____.

Put the yarn on the _____.

Then knit.

Use a _____ and measure the scarf.

Continue knitting until the scarf is long and just right.

B. *Write about the project for your assignment.*

1. What tools do you need?_____

2. What supplies do you need?_____

Tip for Writers

Time-Order Words. Remember that ordinal numbers order the steps for your reader. *Time-order* words also order the steps for your reader. Use both in your writing about a process. Here are some examples. Use a comma after these words.

First,	*Then,*	*After that,*
First of all,	*Next,*	*Finally,*
Second,		

A. *Add time-order words to these steps for making a pretty flower pot.*

Example:

First of all, knit the yarn.

1. _____ put the pot in the middle.

2. _____ cover the pot with the knitting.

3. _____ glue the knitting to the pot.

4. _____ glue buttons to the knitting.

B. *Add time-order words to your sentences about your project on page 32.*

Focused Practice

A. *Read the sentences and answer the questions on page 35.*

> I make my own window cleaner.
>
> You can make window cleaner yourself too.
>
> There are many ways to make it.
>
> Here's one simple way.
>
> First, you measure 1 cup of water.
>
> Pour it into a bottle.
>
> Add ½ measuring cup of vinegar and ½ cup of rubbing alcohol.
>
> Add 1 small spoonful of lemon juice.
>
> After that, mix it all very well.
>
> Finally, add 1 more cup of water.
>
> Now you are ready to clean your windows.

1. What is the do-it-yourself project? Circle the project.

2. Count the sentences. How many are there? _____

3. Do the sentences answer at least two of these questions? Check (✓) the questions.

   ☐ What is the first step in the process?

   ☐ What is the second step?

   ☐ What is the last step?

4. Does every imperative sentence have a verb? Do the other sentences have a subject and verb? Underline the subjects and verbs.

5. Circle the capital letters in the sentences. Circle the period at the end of each sentence.

B. *Work with a partner. Compare your answers.*

Your Own Writing

Revising Your Draft

A. *Look at your sentences on page 32, Writing for the Assignment. Then read the Revision Checklist and check (✓) your answers. What do you need to revise?*

B. *Revise your sentences. Add steps when needed.*

Revision Checklist	Yes	No
1. Circle the project in your sentences. Are all the sentences about the project?		
2. Count the sentences. Are there at least five sentences?		
3. Do your sentences answer these questions?		
• What is the first step in the process?		
• What is the second step?		
• What is the last step?		
4. Underline the subject and verb in the sentences. Does every imperative sentence have a verb?		
Do all other sentences have a subject and a verb?		
5. Circle the capital letters in the sentences. Circle the period at the end of each sentence. Are the sentences correct?		

Step 4 Editing

■ GRAMMAR PRESENTATION

Before you hand in your sentences, look at your sentences one more time and edit them. In this editing section, you review the simple present of verbs. Think about your sentences as you review.

Simple Present: Statements

Grammar Notes	Examples
1. Use the **simple present** to talk about facts or things that happen again and again.	• Hal **is** an inventor. (*a fact*) • The Maker Faire **happens** once a year. (*a thing that happens again and again*)
2. In **affirmative statements**, use the **base form** of the verb with *I*, *you*, *we*, and *they*. Add *-s* or *-es* only with the third-person singular (*he, she, it*). Add *-s* to most verbs. Add *-es* to verbs that end in *ch*, *o*, *ss*, *sh*, *x*, or *z*.	• I **play** the guitar. • They **build** cars. • He **makes** bread. • She **fixes** bicycles.
3. Use *do not* or *does not* + **the base form of the verb** to make a **negative** statement. We often use the contractions *don't* and *doesn't* in speaking and informal writing.	• They **do not live** near a Maker Faire. • He **does not like** DIY projects. • They **don't understand** the instructions. • He **doesn't have** a hammer.
4. *Be* and *have* are irregular verbs. *Be* has three forms in the present: *am, is, are*. *Have* has two forms: *have, has*.	• I **am** a DIYer. My brother **is** a DIYer too. • I **have** a lot of project ideas. Kim **has** some good ideas too.

Focused Practice

A. *Read the sentences. Circle the subject. Underline the simple present form of the verb.*

Example:

(I) do not make things from scratch.

1. I am not a DIYer.

2. They are DIYers.

3. They grow vegetables in their garden.

4. They put the fresh vegetables in a pot.

5. Then, they add water.

6. They make homemade soup themselves.

7. It tastes delicious.

B. *Complete the sentences with the correct form of the simple present verb.*

1. My dad _____ (**make**) cars.

2. The cars _____ (**come**) in parts.

3. First, he _____ (**check**) the parts.

4. His neighbor _____ (**watch**).

5. Then they _____ (**build**) the car together.

C. *Correct the use of the simple present verb in the sentences. Add a subject when it is missing from the sentence.*

Example:

I likes to go to parties. *I like to go to parties.* _____

1. I likes to give parties. _____

2. First, you invites people. _____

3. Next, cleans your house. _____

4. Then, puts good music on. _____

5. Finally, you has fun. _____

Your Own Writing

Editing Your Draft

A. *Edit your sentences for the assignment. Use the Editing Checklist below.*

B. *Write a clean copy of your sentences. Give it to your teacher.*

Editing Checklist		
Did you . . .	**Yes**	**No**
• use the simple present of the verbs correctly?		
• use vocabulary from the unit correctly?		
• use capital letters, commas, and periods correctly?		
• use complete sentences?		
• order the steps in a process with correct time-order words?		

UNIT 3 Food

IN THIS UNIT   This unit is about food. What food is interesting to you? What meals are unforgettable?

There is interesting food all over the world. People like different flavors. Some people like very plain food. Others like spicy food. Some people like tasting different kinds of foods from different countries. Some prefer only food from their own countries.

What food do you like?

Planning for Writing

◼ BRAINSTORM

A. Using a Ranking Chart. *Ranking helps you organize things from best to worst. Look at the ranking list. Then use stars and rank the food in the ranking chart below. Discuss your answers with a partner.*

Ranking List	
★★★★★	Delicious
★★★★	Very good
★★★	Good
★★	OK, but not my favorite
★	Not good
0 stars	Never eat this

Ranking Chart	
Food	**Star Ranking**
hamburger	
chicken	
salad	
spaghetti	
chocolate	
cake	

B. *Read the Web reviews for the restaurants. Write the average star ranking for each restaurant.*

The Burger Lounge   Average ranking: ___5 stars___
717 Emerald Bay Rd.

★★★★★ Burger Lounge hamburgers are great! The French fries are crispy and delicious. The milk shakes are creamy and sweet.
Click here for more reviews: ★★★★★ ★★★★★

Thai House   Average ranking: _____
32 Tallac Road

★★★★ If you like Thai food, go to Thai House! They have spicy dishes and mild ones too. Click here for more reviews: ★★★   ★★★★★

Pizza and More   Average ranking: _____
117 Main Street

★ The pizza here was terrible! It was cold and very salty. The spaghetti was OK.
Click here for more reviews: ★   ★

China King   Average ranking: _____
72 Tahoe Blvd.

★★★ The food here is pretty good. The vegetables are very fresh. Everything is tasty. But the pot stickers are a little greasy.
Click here for more reviews: ★★★★   ★★

C. *Read the average ranking of the restaurants in Exercise B. Then look at the ranking chart below. Write the restaurant names in the correct order on the chart.*

Restaurant	Star Ranking	
The Burger Lounge	★★★★★	Delicious
	★★★★	Very good
	★★★	Good
	★★	OK, but not my favorite
	★	Not good
	0 stars	Never eat here

THE RESTAURANT CRITIC

1 Jonathan Gold is a writer. He writes about restaurants in Los Angeles. He is a restaurant critic for the *LA Weekly*. For his job, Gold eats at 300 to 500 restaurants every year and writes about them. Most restaurant critics eat at five-star restaurants, but Gold is not a typical restaurant critic.

2 Gold loves interesting, international food. He writes about taco trucks. He visits tiny Peruvian restaurants in shopping malls. He finds Thai restaurants that do not have menus in English. These restaurants do not have star rankings at all.

3 Los Angeles has a lot of immigrants. The immigrants come from new places every year. So there is always new food for Gold to try.

4 Gold enjoys trying unusual food. He especially enjoys spicy food. When he was a child, Gold loved hot sauce. Now, he orders *really* spicy dishes[1] all the time, not the mild dishes that are typical in the United States.

5 A few of the things Gold writes about are crunchy fried grasshoppers[2] and a delicious drink with worms in it. They are specialties at a Mexican restaurant. In one Chinese

Taco truck

restaurant review, he describes a plate of jellyfish[3] in oil. In another review, he writes about eating sweet *live* prawns[4] and octopus.[5]

6 Sometimes he finds an interesting dessert, such as an avocado[6] milk shake or rich brown-bread ice cream.

7 Some people think spaghetti and pizza are interesting international foods. These people probably do not read Gold's reviews, but thousands of adventurous eaters in Los Angeles read his blog every week and plan for unusual meals.

---

[1] **dishes:** food that you prepare in a particular way

[2] **grasshopper**

[3] **jellyfish**

[4] **prawn**

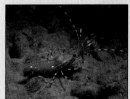

[5] **octopus**

[6] **avocado**

Building Word Knowledge

Opposites. Some adjectives describe food. Many food adjectives have opposites. Learn these words in pairs to remember them well. Here are some opposites.

peppery / salty	*sweet / sour*
plain / fancy	*hot / cold*
spicy / mild	*rich / light*
dry / greasy	*crunchy / creamy*

Look at the pictures. Describe the food. Circle one word in each pair.

Example:

tacos

a. (plain) / fancy

b. (spicy) / mild

c. (greasy) / dry

1. crackers

a. crunchy / creamy

b. peppery / salty

c. fancy / plain

2. salad

a. light / rich

b. plain / fancy

c. hot / cold

3. ice cream sundae

a. rich / light

b. sweet / sour

c. crunchy / creamy

Comprehension

A. *Read "The Restaurant Critic" on page 41 again. Complete the sentences. Circle the correct letter.*

1. Jonathan Gold writes about _____.

   a. restaurants

   b. typical American food

   c. immigrants

2. Gold likes _____ food.

   a. live

   b. expensive

   c. international

3. Gold finds interesting food in Los Angeles because _____.

   a. it is near the ocean, and there is good seafood

   b. many people from other countries live there

   c. there are many spaghetti and pizza restaurants there

4. _____ read Gold's restaurant reviews.

   a. Adventurous eaters

   b. Typical American eaters

   c. Immigrants

B. *Think about the reading. Read the questions and discuss your answers with a partner.*

1. What food does the typical restaurant critic eat? Describe the food.
2. What food does Jonathan Gold like? Describe the food.
3. What food do you like? Describe the food.
4. Is the food you like also the kind of food Jonathan Gold likes? Explain.

Tip for Writers

Short Lists with *And* and *Or*. Writers often put short lists in sentences. When you make a short list, write *and* or *or* between the last two items. Put a comma between the items. Here are some examples.

*Jonathan Gold eats **grasshoppers, prawns, octopus, and jellyfish**.*

*You can have **soda, milk, apple juice, or water**.*

A. *Underline the words in each list. Add commas.*

Example:

Are tacos <u>Mexican</u>, <u>Thai</u>, <u>Chinese</u>, or <u>Brazilian</u>?

1. I don't like carrots potatoes or peas.

2. Jellyfish octopus and prawns come from the ocean.

3. Do you want chocolate mint vanilla strawberry or coffee ice cream?

4. I'm full! I ate turkey potatoes gravy sausages vegetables and chocolate cake.

B. *Complete the sentences. Use the information from the chart and write a short list in each sentence.*

Average Ranking	Restaurant	Adjectives to Describe the Food
★ ★ ★ ★ ★	Paco's Tacos	good, fun, inexpensive
★ ★ ★ ★	Mel's Diner	good, greasy, inexpensive
★ ★ ★ ★	Roma	good, friendly, expensive
★ ★ ★ ★	Noodle House	fun, friendly, inexpensive
★ ★ ★ ↲	Chow	healthy, expensive, tasty
★ ★	Le Charm	fancy, expensive, OK

Example:

Paco's Tacos is *good, fun, and inexpensive*.

1. _____ are three inexpensive restaurants.

2. _____ have four stars.

3. Chow is a _____ restaurant.

4. _____ are good restaurants.

5. Le Charm is _____.

Writing a Paragraph

In this unit, you write a paragraph about food. A **paragraph** is a group of sentences. A paragraph has sentences about one idea. Remember that a sentence is a group of words. Each sentence is a complete idea with a subject and a verb.

Step 1   Prewriting

Prewriting helps you get ideas and helps you prepare to write. In this prewriting, you choose your assignment, write some ideas, and rank the ideas for your assignment.

Your Own Writing

Choosing Your Assignment

A. *Choose Assignment 1 or Assignment 2.*

> **Assignment 1:** Write about your favorite food.

> **Assignment 2:** Write about your favorite dish.

B. *Make a list of food or dishes in the charts below. Write at least five. This will help you choose a food or dish for your assignment. Write a list of adjectives about each one. This will help you describe the food or dish for your assignment.*

Food	Adjectives
avocado	tasty, green, creamy
rice	plain, healthy, light, delicious

Dishes	Adjectives
guacamole	tasty, spicy, rich, Mexican
paella	rich, spicy, greasy, Spanish

C. Checking in. *Share your list of food or dishes with a partner. Describe the items on your list. Ask your partner questions.*

Examples:

Where is each food or dish from?

Is it a traditional food or dish?

Where do you eat it? at home? in a restaurant? on the street?

What is in it? meat? vegetables? spices? fish?

D. *Write your food or dishes in the ranking chart below. Then choose your five-star food or dish for this assignment.*

Food or Dishes	Star Ranking	
	★★★★★	Delicious
	★★★★	Very good
	★★★	Good
	★★	OK, but not my favorite
	★	Not good
	0 stars	Never eat this

Step 2 Writing the First Draft

■ THE TOPIC

A paragraph in English has several sentences. All the sentences are about one idea. The one idea is the **topic** of the paragraph.

Example:

> Macaroni and cheese is my children's favorite food. They call it "mac and cheese." Every day, they want it. It is rich and creamy. I do not think it is very healthy. We only eat it once a week in our house.

The topic of this paragraph is macaroni and cheese. All the sentences in the paragraph are about this one idea.

Focused Practice

A. *Read each paragraph. Circle the topic of each paragraph.*

Paragraph 1

Bocanova is a great restaurant. The food there is from South America. My favorite dish at the restaurant is empanadas. There are also wonderful cheeses from South America at Bocanova.

a. my favorite dish   **b.** the restaurant Bocanova

Paragraph 2

Eggs are the perfect food. They are very healthy, and they taste delicious. There are many ways to cook eggs. You can boil them or fry them. You can make an omelet, or you can bake them. Cooking eggs is always quick, easy, and tasty.

a. eggs   **b.** cooking

B. *Look at the paragraphs in Exercise A. How many sentences are there in each one?*

Pararaph 1 _____ sentences

Pararaph 2 _____ sentences

Building Word Knowledge

Suffix -ed with Cooking Adjectives. Some adjectives describe the way you cook food. Add -ed to the end of a cooking verb to make these adjectives. Cooking adjectives can help you write about the food and dishes you like. Here are some examples.

Verb	Adjective	Verb	Adjective
boil	boiled	steam	steamed
bake	baked	roast	roasted

A. *Work in a group. Match the adjectives with their definitions. Use your dictionary for help.*

1. _____ baked   **a.** cooked in hot water

2. _____ boiled   **b.** cooked slowly in sauce

3. _____ cooked   **c.** cooked in oil

4. _____ fried   **d.** not raw

5. _____ steamed   **e.** cooked above very hot water

6. _____ stewed   **f.** cooked in the oven

7. _____ broiled   **g.** cooked under direct heat

B. *Look at the foods below. What is your favorite way to cook or eat these foods? Discuss your answers with a partner.*

Example:

fish: *I like broiled, steamed, and baked fish. I don't really like fried fish.*

1. carrots   **2.** chicken   **3.** eggs   **4.** fish   **5.** potatoes

Tip for Writers

Short Lists. Writers often put short lists in sentences. When you make a short list, be sure that all the items in the list are the same part of speech. Remember to use commas between the items. Here are some examples.

*I need **milk, fish, spices,** and **salt**.* (all nouns)

*The soup is **rich, spicy,** and **delicious**.* (all adjectives)

A. *Cross out the item that is not the same part of speech as the other words in each list.*

Example:

I like to cook, eat, ~~vegetables~~, and bake.

1. Eggs are delicious, easy, salt, tasty, and healthy.

2. Jonathan loves sour, milk shakes, fish, and ice cream.

3. Bibimbap is spicy, healthy, vegetables, and colorful.

4. Meat, fish, healthy, and vegetables are good for you.

B. *Combine each pair of sentences. Use a list in your new sentence.*

Example:

Charlie likes McDonald's. Jamal and Daisuke like McDonald's too.

Charlie, Jamal, and Daisuke like McDonald's.

1. This peanut butter is sticky and rich. It is crunchy too.

_____

2. Tangerines are delicious winter fruits. Apples and pomegranates are good in winter too.

_____

3. Please buy milk and butter at the store. Oh, and buy some bread too.

_____

4. These grapes are sweet. They are fresh and juicy too.

_____

C. *Complete each sentence with a list. Be sure all the items in each list are the same part of speech.*

Example:

My favorite foods are *lasagna*, *roast chicken*, and *pizza*.

1. I don't like _____ , _____ , _____ , or _____ .

2. Ice cream is _____ , _____ , and _____ .

3. Please buy _____ , _____ , _____ , and _____ at the grocery store.

4. I think hamburgers are _____ , _____ , and _____ .

Your Own Writing

Finding Out More

A. *Go online. Type the keyword [the name of your food or dish]. Find information about the food or dish for your assignment. Find information about another interesting food or dish too.*

B. *Write the name of your food or dishes. Answer the questions.*

	Food or Dish Name _____	Food or Dish Name _____
Where is the food or dish from?		
Is it a popular food or dish?		
What adjectives describe it?		
What food do you eat with it?		
When do you eat it?		
What do you make with this food? OR What is in the dish?		
Other interesting information:		

C. **Checking in.** *Share your information about the food or dishes with a partner. Add ideas you like from your partner's list.*

Planning Your Paragraph

A. *Look at the food or dishes in your chart. Choose the food or dish for your assignment. You can choose the food or dish from your ranking chart on page 46, or you can choose from Exercise B above.*

➡

B. Writing for the Assignment. *Write five or more sentences about the food or dish.*

Example:

Hard-boiled eggs are delicious.

People eat hard-boiled eggs hot and cold.

They are good in salads too.

They are very good with a little salt, pepper, and mayonnaise.

My favorite is hard-boiled eggs on toast with butter.

_____

_____

_____

_____

Step 3 Revising

Paragraphs in English have a special format. They begin with an indent. Then the sentences follow each other on the same line. Each sentence begins with a capital letter and ends with the correct punctuation. Always correct the paragraph format when you revise.

■ INDENTING PARAGRAPHS

Leave a small space before the first sentence in each paragraph. This space is an **indent**. Indenting tells your reader that you are starting a new paragraph with a new idea.

Here is a short paragraph about hard-boiled eggs. Notice the indent.

Example:

Hard-boiled eggs are very healthy. People eat hard-boiled eggs hot and cold. Sometimes people cut the eggs and add them to salads. Sometimes people mix the eggs with mayonnaise. This makes a creamy mixture. Some people add pickles. Then the mixture is a little crunchy and a little sour. They spread the mixture on bread and make sandwiches. It is delicious and good for you.

Focused Practice

A. Check (✓) the paragraphs that are indented correctly.

a. _____ Trader's Grocery is a wonderful grocery store. They have a lot of specially prepared dishes there. You can buy very good frozen pizza with tomatoes and basil, homemade mozzarella cheese, salty capers, and fancy herbs. They have a spicy spaghetti sauce in a jar. They have excellent frozen tamales in a rich tomato sauce. It is the perfect store with perfectly wonderful dishes to take home.

b. _____ Trader's Grocery is a wonderful grocery store. They have a lot of specially prepared dishes there. You can buy very good frozen pizza with tomatoes and basil, homemade mozzarella cheese, salty capers, and fancy herbs. They have a spicy spaghetti sauce in a jar. They have excellent frozen tamales in a rich tomato sauce. It is the perfect store with perfectly wonderful dishes to take home.

c. _____ Trader's Grocery is a wonderful grocery store. They have a lot of specially prepared dishes there. You can buy very good frozen pizza with tomatoes and basil, homemade mozzarella cheese, salty capers, and fancy herbs. They have a spicy spaghetti sauce in a jar. They have excellent frozen tamales in a rich tomato sauce. It is the perfect store with perfectly wonderful dishes to take home.

d. _____ Trader's Grocery is a wonderful grocery store. They have a lot of specially prepared dishes there. You can buy very good frozen pizza with tomatoes and basil, homemade mozzarella cheese, salty capers, and fancy herbs. They have a spicy spaghetti sauce in a jar. They have excellent frozen tamales in a rich tomato sauce. It is the perfect store with perfectly wonderful dishes to take home.

B. Write these sentences as a correct paragraph. Indent the first sentence.

French fries are popular everywhere. Almost every country makes French fries. Good fries are crispy outside, soft inside, not greasy, and not dry. Some people eat them with vinegar. Some people eat them with ketchup. Some people like them salty. I like them plain and hot.

_____

_____

_____

_____

_____

■ SPACING

A paragraph is a group of sentences. The sentences are not in a list. They follow each other on the same line when possible. There is one space after each sentence. Compare the list and the paragraph below.

A list of sentences about Spettro

Spettro is a great pizza restaurant.

They make their own traditional sauces.

They make their own pizza crust.

They use really good cheese.

Their pizza is the best.

A paragraph about Spettro

Spettro is a great pizza restaurant. They make their own traditional sauces and their own pizza crust. They also use really good cheese. Their pizza is the best.

Focused Practice

Make a slash (/) between the sentences in the paragraph.

Paragraph 1

Bibimbap is a typical Korean dish. / Bibimbap is warm white rice with cooked fresh vegetables. Sometimes the vegetables are spicy. There is usually meat or plain tofu on top of the rice. A raw egg is a common addition. It is always colorful, and it is very delicious.

Paragraph 2

Potatoes are my favorite food. They are a popular food throughout the world. They are healthy. They taste good, and they are easy to cook. I like them boiled, steamed, and fried. I like stewed potatoes in dishes with meat and other vegetables. Plain baked potatoes are especially delicious with a little bit of butter, salt, and cheese.

Building Word Knowledge

The Prefix *Un-*. A prefix is something you add to the beginning of a word. It changes the meaning of the word.

Un- is a prefix. It means *not*. For example, *uncommon* means *not common*. Study the following adjectives with *un-*.

uncommon (not common)   *unusual* (not usual)

unpopular (not popular)   *unhealthy* (not healthy)

untraditional (not traditional) *unforgettable* (not forgettable)

unfamiliar (not familiar)

A. *Complete the sentences. Circle the correct adjective.*

Example:

French fries are very (**common** / **uncommon**) in most of the world.

1. Cola is a very (**popular** / **unpopular**) drink.

2. Wow! Peanut butter pizza! That is (**traditional** / **untraditional**).

3. Sammy eats the same thing every day. He doesn't like

   (**familiar** / **unfamiliar**) food.

4. Jonathan Gold likes (**usual** / **unusual**) dishes.

5. Vegetables are very (**healthy** / **unhealthy**).

6. *L'Escargot* is a five-star restaurant. The meals there are always

   (**forgettable** / **unforgettable**).

B. *Write true sentences. Use the highlighted adjectives and the prefix* un-.

Example:

Bagels are common in New York.

Bagels are uncommon in Casablanca.

1. Salty fish is very popular in Norway.

   _____

2. Fish and rice is a very traditional dish in Cape Verde.

   _____

3. Mexican food is familiar to people in Texas.

   _____

4. Pad thai is a common dish in Thai restaurants.

   _____

C. Writing for the Assignment. *Look at your sentences on page 50, Writing for the Assignment. Write your sentences as a correct paragraph. Remember to indent the first sentence. Use Building Word Knowledge words, if possible.*

   _____

   _____

   _____

   _____

   _____

■ CAPITALIZATION AND PUNCTUATION

Sentences always begin with a capital letter. They always end with a period, exclamation point, or question mark.

Punctuation Notes	Examples
1. Use a **period (.)** at the end of most sentences.	• I like baked potatoes. • Oatmeal cookies are my favorite.
2. Use a **question mark (?)** at the end of questions.	• Do you prefer boiled potatoes? • What kind of cookies do you like?
3. Use an **exclamation point (!)** to show surprise or excitement.	• Anne made potato salad with raw potatoes! • That bakery has pepper cookies!

Focused Practice

A. *Circle the capital letter at the beginning of each sentence. Circle the punctuation at the end of each sentence.*

Breakfast at Sue's Bed and Breakfast is always delicious. She usually makes baked pancakes with stewed fruit. Her fried potatoes are always crispy and delicious. There are always hard-boiled eggs and toast. You can eat as much as you want! Do you want to come to breakfast at Sue's?

B. *Correct the paragraph. Add capital letters and punctuation.*

turducken is an unusual dish it is popular in the south of the United States some people eat the traditional turkey at Thanksgiving some untraditional families eat turducken what is turducken this dish is a chicken in a duck in a roasted turkey it makes a delicious, unforgettable meal

Tip for Writers

Descriptive Adjectives. Descriptive adjectives make your writing more interesting. Compare the following sentences. The second sentence is more interesting. It includes descriptive adjectives and gives more details.

They make their own sauces.

They make their own rich and creamy sauces.

A. *Circle the sentence in each pair that gives more information.*

1. a. Sue usually makes baked pancakes with stewed fruit.

   b. Sue usually makes light, hot, baked pancakes with sweet, stewed fruit.

2. a. Her spicy, fried potatoes are always crisp and delicious.

   b. Her fried potatoes are always delicious.

3. a. There are always boiled eggs and toast.

   b. There are always fresh boiled eggs and homemade toast.

B. *Work with a partner. Rewrite the sentences. Add descriptive adjectives.*

1. My friend makes his own bread.

_____

2. My favorite dish is salad.

_____

3. I love candy.

_____

■ REVISING THE PARAGRAPH

Revising your own paragraph means you make changes and make your writing better. Pay attention to paragraph format, capitalization, and punctuation every time you revise.

Focused Practice

A. *Read the paragraph and answer the questions.*

> Bananas are a very popular fruit in many places. They are delicious, sweet, and easy to eat. I eat them plain or on my cereal in the morning. Sometimes I make baked bananas, fried bananas, or banana bread. Often I eat them for a snack at school. Some people think they are unhealthy and make you fat. I think they are healthy and good.

(continued)

1. What food or dish does the paragraph describe? Circle the food or dish.

2. Count the sentences. How many are there? _____

3. Does the writer do these things to format the paragraph? Check (✓) the things the writer does.

   ☐ Indents the first sentence of the paragraph

   ☐ Uses one space between sentences

   ☐ Writes sentences on the same line when possible

   ☐ Uses capital letters and correct punctuation

4. Are there at least three new vocabulary words or phrases from this unit? Underline them.

B. *Work with a partner. Compare your answers.*

Your Own Writing

Revising Your Draft

A. *Look at your paragraph on page 53. Writing for the Assignment. Then read the Revision Checklist and check (✓) your answers. What do you need to revise?*

B. *Revise your paragraph. Add descriptive adjectives when possible. They make your reading more interesting.*

Revision Checklist	Yes	No
1. Circle the food or dish your paragraph describes. Are all the sentences about this food or dish?		
2. Count the sentences. Are there at least five sentences?		
3. Did you do all of the following in your paragraph?		
• indent the first sentence of the paragraph?		
• use one space between sentences?		
• write sentences on the same line when possible?		
• use capital letters and correct punctuation?		
• include a subject and a verb in each sentence?		
4. Put a star (*) next to each new word or phrase from this unit. Did you include at least three new words?		

■ GRAMMAR PRESENTATION

Before you hand in your paragraph, edit it and look for errors in punctuation, capitalization, and grammar. In this editing section, you review adjective and noun modifiers. Think about your paragraph as you review.

Noun and Adjective Modifiers

Grammar Notes	Examples
1. Adjectives can **modify (describe) nouns**. They give more information about a noun.	*adjective noun* • Jonathan likes **spicy food**.
Nouns can also **modify nouns**.	*noun noun* • Paella is a **rice dish**.
2. Adjectives can come **after the verb** *be* or **before a noun**.	• He is **adventurous**. • He is an **adventurous eater**.
3. **Do not add** *-s* to an adjective or a noun modifier.	• He wants a **spicy** pepper. • He likes **spicy** peppers. • He wants a **cheese** sandwich. • He likes **cheese** sandwiches. Not: He likes ~~spicys~~ peppers. He likes ~~cheeses~~ sandwiches.
4. Before a **singular count noun**: Use *a* before a modifier that begins with a **consonant sound**. Use *an* before a modifier that begins with a **vowel sound**.	• That's **a yellow** tomato. • That's **a delicious** peach. • That's **an unusual** fruit.
5. When both an **adjective** and a **noun** modify a noun, the **adjective** comes **first**.	• This is a **good cheese** sandwich. • This is a **salty chicken** dish.

Focused Practice

A. *Read the sentences. Circle the adjective and noun modifiers. Underline the nouns.*

Example:

Chicken Tikka Masala is a (delicious chicken) <u>dish</u>.

1. In Brazil, people eat heavy, cheesy bread balls called *pão de queijo*.

2. We had a wonderful spaghetti dinner last night.

3. Do you have a recipe for that rich, creamy mushroom soup?

4. "Jerk chicken" is a spicy dish from Jamaica.

5. Pho is a light noodle soup from Vietnam.

B. *Rewrite the sentences. Add the modifiers in the correct order.*

Example:

Steve loves pizza. (**pepperoni**)

Steve loves pepperoni pizza.

1. Bibimbap is a dish from Korea. (**traditional**)

   _____

2. "Maffe sauce" is a sauce in dishes from West Africa. (**peanut**) (**popular**)

   _____

3. Gazpacho is a soup. (**healthy**) (**vegetable**).

   _____

4. Umm Ali is a dessert from Egypt. (**creamy**) (**holiday**)

   _____

C. *Correct the sentences.*

Example:

I like chicken plain sandwiches.

I like plain chicken sandwiches.

1. I want an hot cup of tea.

   _____

2. These cookies are very sweets.

   _____

3. You can have chickens kebabs or vegetables kebabs.

   _____

4. This is an juicy orange.

   _____

5. I love spicy cheeses sandwiches.

   _____

Your Own Writing

Editing Your Draft

A. *Edit your paragraph for the assignment. Use the Editing Checklist below.*

B. *Write a clean copy of your paragraph. Give it to your teacher.*

Editing Checklist		
Did you . . .	**Yes**	**No**
• use noun and adjective modifiers correctly?		
• indent the paragraph correctly?		
• use correct capital letters and end punctuation?		
• use complete sentences?		
• describe the food or dish in an interesting way?		
• include short lists with commas and the correct parts of speech?		

UNIT 4 Clothes

IN THIS UNIT   This unit is about clothes. What clothes do you like? Why do you like them?

Some people say: "Clothes make the man." Our clothes send a message. They tell who we are or who we want to be. Some clothes say, "Look at me!" Some clothes say, "I have a lot of money!" Some clothes say, "I am not like everyone else." Even if you don't pay attention to your clothes, you are sending a message.

Do you agree? How do you choose clothes?

Planning for Writing

BRAINSTORM

A. *Read about one of the photos.*

Sally likes to be different. She always wears black. She likes black leather boots and jackets. She almost always wears tight black jeans and a black leather belt. She often wears dark glasses.

a. b. c.

Read the questions. Discuss your answers with a partner.

1. Which picture does the paragraph describe: a, b, or c?

2. What words describe the clothes?

B. Using a Cluster Chart. *Cluster charts help you get ideas and organize information. Look at the cluster chart below. What information in the paragraph in Exercise A is from the chart? Circle the information in the paragraph in Exercise A.*

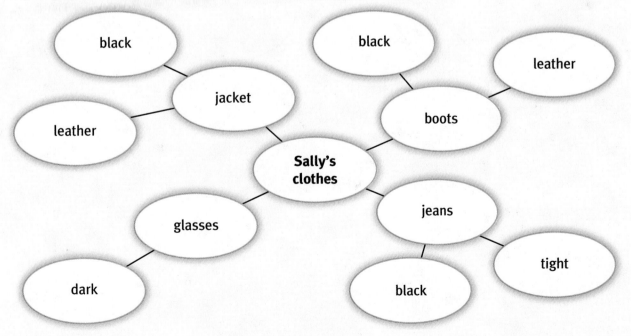

C. *Read the paragraph. A cluster chart helped the writer get ideas. Complete the writer's cluster chart.*

    Donald wears classic suits and conservative ties. He usually wears dark color suits in blue, black, or gray. His shirts are white. His shoes are very trendy.[1] He always wears clothes that say, "I am a success."

[1] **trendy:** fashionable; in the style that is popular now

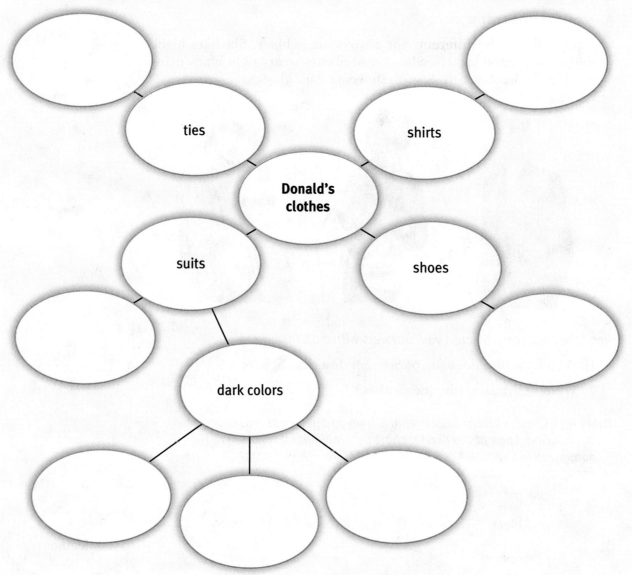

Read the article about baseball caps.

Baseball Caps for Everyone

1   The president of the United States wears them. Fashion models wear them. Retired men wear them to go fishing. Little girls wear them. Little boys wear them. People in Japan wear them. Brazilians wear them. And, yes, baseball players wear them too.

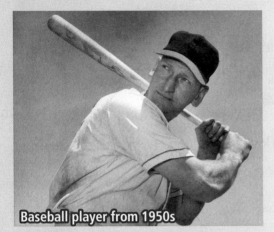

Baseball player from 1950s

2   Baseball caps are everywhere. How did they become so popular?

3   Baseball players began wearing baseball caps in the 1950s. Soon, baseball fans[1] began wearing baseball caps with their favorite team logo[2] on them.

4   In the 1960s salespeople[3] began using baseball caps to advertise[4] things. For example, tractor[5] salespeople gave away free caps with the John Deere tractor logo. Truck drivers wore the free John Deere caps.

5   Today, almost everyone likes baseball caps. They are practical, light, comfortable, and easy to carry everywhere. Perhaps most importantly, baseball caps keep the sun away from your face and eyes.

6   Some people like baseball caps for another reason. These people sometimes wear their caps backwards, or they wear them inside the house. These people don't need a practical cap. They wear baseball caps because they are fashionable.

7   Many caps are still free, but some caps you buy. Today, almost any place you visit has baseball caps for sale. They are usually not very expensive. In New York you can buy an "I ♥ NY" cap. At Disneyland, you can buy a Disneyland baseball cap. But for some designer caps, you can pay a lot of money. Some popular singers and actors love the modern Elita baseball cap. It has a real gold[6] button on it, fits perfectly, and costs $2,000!

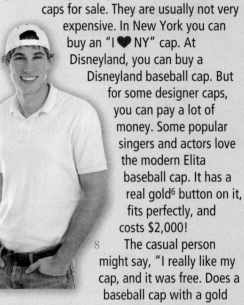

8   The casual person might say, "I really like my cap, and it was free. Does a baseball cap with a gold button keep the sun off your face better than my cap?" But for the trendy person who wears his or her hat backwards, the answer is easy: "It doesn't matter. It's just for fashion."

---

[1] **fan:** someone who likes a particular person or thing very much

[2] **logo:** a picture that is the official sign of a company or organization

[3] **salespeople:** people whose job is to sell things

[4] **advertise:** to try to make people buy things using pictures and words

[5] **tractor:** a strong vehicle with large wheels that is used on farms

[6] **gold:** expensive yellow-colored metal

Building Word Knowledge

Synonyms. Some words have a similar meaning. These are synonyms. Learn synonyms together. You will remember them better. Here are some synonyms about fashion.

fashionable — trendy   simple — plain

old-fashioned — out of date   dressy — formal

practical — useful   everyday — casual

classic — conservative   tailored — well-fitted

Complete the sentences. Use synonyms for the highlighted words.

Example:

You can wear everyday clothes to the party. It's a _____*casual*_____ party.

1. Elisa always wears simple dresses. Her shoes are _____ too.

2. This jacket is very practical in the snow and _____ in the rain.

3. I usually wear classic suits to work. We need to wear _____ clothes there.

4. My grandfather gave me an old-fashioned suit. The shoes he gave me are _____ too.

5. The wedding is very formal. Wear something _____.

6. I like well-fitted jackets. I look good in _____ clothes.

Comprehension

A. *Read "Baseball Caps for Everyone" on page 63 again. Cross out the incorrect answer to each question.*

1. How did baseball caps become so popular?

   a. Baseball fans wore caps for their favorite team.

   b. Salespeople gave them away for free.

   c. The president wore them.

   d. Baseball players wore them.

2. Why are baseball caps very practical?

   a. They are light.

   b. They are easy to carry.

   c. They can be very expensive.

   d. They keep the sun off of your eyes and face.

B. *Read the article again. There are many opinions. Check (✓) the opinions from the article. Then, give your own opinion. Circle* I agree. *or* I don't agree.

Example:

<u> ✓ </u> Almost everyone loves baseball caps.

(I agree.)   I don't agree.

_____ **1.** Baseball caps are practical.

    I agree.   I don't agree.

_____ **2.** Baseball caps are popular everywhere.

    I agree.   I don't agree.

_____ **3.** Baseball caps are fashionable.

    I agree.   I don't agree.

_____ **4.** Backwards baseball caps are out-of-date.

    I agree.   I don't agree.

_____ **5.** Baseball caps are casual.

    I agree.   I don't agree.

C. *Think about the reading. Read the questions and discuss your answers with a partner. Use the ideas in the box or your own ideas.*

a fan	a young girl	your teacher	you
a famous actress	your friend	a writer	

1. Who probably wears this baseball cap?

2. Who probably has this cup?

3. Who probably buys this cap?

Writing a Paragraph

In this unit, you write a paragraph about clothes. Remember: A paragraph includes a group of sentences about one idea, that is, the topic. The first sentence usually tells the topic. It is the topic sentence.

Step 1   Prewriting

Prewriting helps you get ideas and prepare to write. In this prewriting, you choose your assignment. Then you make a cluster chart.

Building Word Knowledge

Word Categories. You can use many nouns and adjectives together to describe clothing. You use them in a certain order to describe different things about the clothing. Read the list of words and the sentences. Notice the order of the adjectives and nouns.

Adjectives	Nouns	Nouns
How does it feel?	**What is it made of?**	**What is it for?**
soft	cotton	work
itchy	wool	play
big	leather	baseball
comfortable	silk	evening
tight	nylon	rain

My **big** boots	My **big leather** boots	My **work** boots
My **leather** boots	My **leather work** boots	My **big leather work** boots

Rewrite the sentences. Describe the clothing. Add the adjectives or nouns in the correct order.

Example:

My handbag is small and practical. (**leather**) (**soft**)

My soft leather handbag is small and practical.

1. My boots are my favorite piece of clothing. (**big**) (**nylon**) (**rain**)

   _____

2. I don't like this sweater. (**wool**) (**itchy**)

   _____

3. I want a dress. (**evening**) (**silk**)

_____

4. He likes pants. (**work**) (**cotton**) (**soft**)

_____

5. I really like my cap. (**baseball**) (**comfortable**) (**nylon**)

_____

6. This scarf is my favorite. (**cotton**)

_____

Your Own Writing

Choosing Your Assignment

A. _Choose Assignment 1 or Assignment 2._

Assignment 1: Write about your favorite piece of clothing.

Assignment 2: Write about a practical piece of clothing.

B. _Make a list of your favorite or practical pieces of clothing. Write at least five items. This will help you choose the item for your assignment._

Favorite Items	Practical Items
red scarf	hiking boots

C. Checking in. _Share your list of clothing with a partner. Ask your partner questions. Add clothing you like to your list._

Examples:

Why is it your favorite? OR How is it practical?

When do you wear it?

Where do you wear it? at home? at work? on the street?

What does it look like? Is it trendy? Is it classic?

D. *Choose one piece of clothing for your assignment. Write the name in the center circle of the cluster chart. Write descriptions of the clothing in the other circles.*

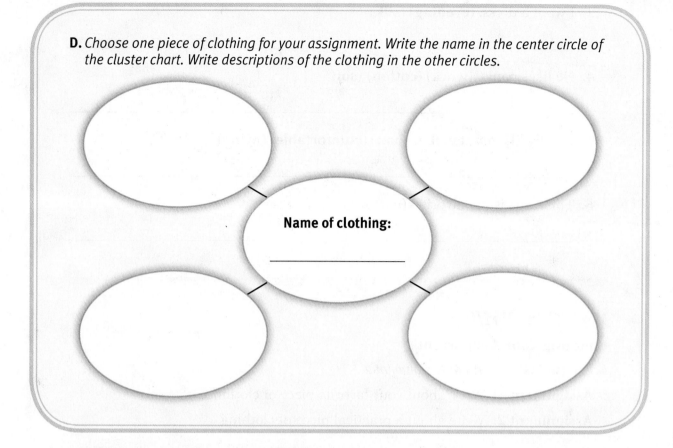

Name of clothing:

_____

Step 2   Writing the First Draft

■ THE TOPIC SENTENCE

The **topic sentence** is usually the first sentence in a paragraph. It introduces the topic. It helps the reader understand what the paragraph is about. All the sentences in the paragraph are about the topic.

Example:

> I have a very special piece of clothing. It is my gray wool formal jacket. I usually do not like dressy clothes, but this jacket is special. It has a classic style. My grandfather bought it for me. It is very comfortable, and it looks great. It also makes me think of my grandfather.

The topic sentence of this paragraph is: *I have a very special piece of clothing.*

All the sentences in the paragraph are about the writer's special piece of clothing, the formal jacket.

Focused Practice

A. *Read each paragraph. Underline the topic sentence. Then circle the answer.*

Paragaph 1

   My favorite black scarf is practical and fashionable. It keeps my neck warm. I wrap it around my head, and it keeps my ears warm too. When I want to take a nap, I put it over my eyes. It keeps the light away from my eyes. It is black, so I can wear it with any other color. It is very easy to carry with me because it is small. I take it everywhere!

What is the paragraph about?

a. the reasons I like my black scarf   **b.** the way I take a nap

Paragaph 2

   My favorite T-shirt is very old, but I love it. It is a simple white cotton T-shirt with a Seneca Lake Summer Camp logo on it. The T-shirt is very old and tight now. It has two small holes in it, but it does not matter. The T-shirt makes me happy because I loved that camp.

What is the paragraph about?

a. the reasons I like my summer camp   **b.** the reasons I like my T-shirt

B. *Read each paragraph. Check (✓) the best topic sentence. Then write the topic sentence in the paragraph.*

Paragraph 1

_____

A cork hat is a traditional Australian sun hat with corks. Australians tie corks to the rim of the hat with string. When they move their head, the corks move. This looks silly, but the corks keep the flies away from their face and head.

_____ **a.** Cork hats are practical in Australia.

_____ **b.** Australians need sun hats.

Paragraph 2

_____

She knit a lovely traditional Norwegian sweater for me. She also made me wool mittens and a colorful wool hat. I often wear all of those things, but my favorite item from her is a pair of wool slippers. They keep my feet warm every night.

_____ **a.** Knit clothing is practical and beautiful.

_____ **b.** My aunt knits a lot of wonderful clothes for me.

C. *Read each paragraph. Write a topic sentence.*

Paragraph 1

_____

They are my favorite everyday jeans because they are very comfortable and soft. They are a little out of date, but I like them anyway.

Paragraph 2

_____

You can wear flip-flops at the beach. You can walk a long way in them. Your feet never get hot. You can also wear fancy flip-flops to parties.

Paragraph 3

_____

It is a beautiful wedding dress. A dressmaker in New York is making it for her. It is very simple and very soft. I think it is silk.

D. *Work in a group. Share your topic sentences from Exercise C. Which ones help the reader understand the paragraph? Why?*

E. Writing for the Assignment. *Think about your topic. Write a topic sentence for your assignment.*

■ THE TOPIC SENTENCE AND CONTROLLING IDEA

The **topic sentence** in a paragraph usually has two parts: the **topic** and the **controlling idea**. The topic tells the reader what the paragraph is about. The controlling idea tells the reader what the paragraph will say about the topic.

Example:

Topic Sentence: My black leather boots are very practical shopping shoes.

Topic: My black leather boots

Controlling Idea: They are very practical shopping shoes.

Focused Practice

A. *Circle the controlling idea for each topic sentence.*

1. <u>My black leather belt</u> is a simple belt, but it is perfect.

   a. The leather is simple.

   b. Black is the perfect color.

   c. The belt is simple, but perfect.

2. <u>My favorite scarf</u> is practical and fashionable.

   a. It's my favorite.

   b. It's both practical and fashionable.

   c. It's useful.

3. People need <u>different shoes</u> for different kinds of work.

 a. Workers need a lot of shoes.

 b. The shoes are different for different jobs.

 c. People need shoes for the beach, parties, work, and other things.

B. *Underline the topic in the topic sentences. Circle the controlling ideas.*

Example:

<u>Cork hats</u> are (practical in Australia).

 1. My favorite T-shirt is very old, but I love it.

 2. Baseball caps are popular all over the world.

 3. My favorite casual sweater shows my personality.

 4. I do not like business suits because they are very formal.

C. *Look at your topic sentence on page 70, Writing for the Assignment. Underline the topic and circle the controlling idea in your topic sentence. Write two more possible topic sentences below. Underline the topic and circle the controlling idea in each sentence.*

1. _____

 _____

2. _____

 _____

Tip for Writers

Paragraph Titles. Titles tell the reader about the paragraph. The title of the paragraph and the topic sentence are often related. Sometimes the title is the same as the topic in the topic sentence.

Always capitalize the first letter and all the important words in a title. Do not capitalize articles (*a, an, the*) or prepositions (*in, from, on*) unless they are the first word in the title.

A. *Circle the capital letters in each paragraph title.*

 1. My First Pair of Boots

 2. My Favorite Pajamas

 3. A Skirt from South Africa

 4. Flip-Flops for the Beach

 5. Every Man Needs a Tuxedo

B. *Correct the paragraph titles. Add capital letters.*

1. my grandma's handmade sweater

2. my practical high heel shoes

3. the bookbag I always carry

4. my favorite shirt in the world

5. a formal wedding gown

C. *Match the titles and the topic sentences.*

1. Good Hiking Boots

2. The Best Shopping Shoes

3. Shoes for Every Job

4. My Two Pairs of Shoes

5. The Best Shoes

_____ **a.** People need different shoes for different kinds of work.

_____ **b.** I only wear flip-flops and boots.

_____ **c.** You need good strong walking shoes in the mountains.

_____ **d.** My black leather shoes are simple, but they are the best shoes I have.

_____ **e.** My black leather boots are perfect shoes for walking in the mall.

Your Own Writing

Finding Out More

A. *Go online. Type the keyword* [name of your clothing]. *Find information about the clothing for your assignment. Find information about another piece of clothing too.*

B. *Write the names of the clothing in the chart. Answer the questions.*

	Name of the Clothing _____	**Name of the Clothing** _____
Where is it from?		
What is it like? Is it trendy? practical? old-fashioned? classic?		
Where do you wear it?		
What is it made of?		
Is it a popular piece of clothing?		
Other interesting information:		

➡

C. Checking in. *Share your information about the clothing with a partner. Add information about other clothing you like from your partner's list.*

Planning Your Paragraph

A. *Look at the clothing in your chart. Choose the clothing for your assignment. You can choose the clothing in your cluster chart on page 68, or you can choose clothing from your chart in Exercise B on page 72.*

B. Writing for the Assignment. *Use your topic sentence, your cluster chart, and your Finding Out More chart. Write a paragraph about the piece of clothing for your assignment. Give your paragraph a title.*

Example:

My Practical Black Leather Boots

My black leather boots are very practical shopping shoes. They are soft and comfortable. I can walk in them for a long time. I can also wear them with different kinds of clothing. They look good with jeans, and they look good with skirts too. I really like my black leather boots!

_____

_____

_____

_____

_____

_____

_____

_____

Step 3   Revising

Revising is the next important step in writing a paragraph. You make changes and make your writing better when you revise. For example, you add new words and ideas. You correct the format of your paragraph too.

Building Word Knowledge

Expressions with *Keep*. Clothing often protects people. Use the word *keep* to describe how clothing protects people. Notice how to use *keep* with clothing.

Clothing		Part of Body	Adjective
Mittens		*my hands*	*cozy.*
Scarves		*my neck*	*warm.*
Wool hats	**keep**	*my head*	*protected.*
Rain boots		*my feet*	*dry.*
Baseball caps		*me*	*cool.*

A. *Complete the sentences. Use the words in the box.*

feet	~~hands~~	head	me	neck

Example:

Mittens keep my _____*hands*_____ warm.

1. These flip-flops keep my _____ cool.

2. This umbrella keeps _____ nice and dry.

3. My wool scarves keep my _____ warm and cozy.

4. These baseball caps keep my _____ protected.

B. *Read the questions. Discuss your answers with a partner.*

1. What other clothing keeps you warm?

2. What other clothing keeps you dry?

3. What kind of clothing keeps you cool?

4. Does the clothing for your assignment keep you cozy, cool, dry, or protected?

Tip for Writers

Paragraph Titles. A good title tells the reader a little about the paragraph. Remember that titles have special capitalization rules. Here are some other rules for titles.

- Titles are short.
- Titles are about the topic.
- Titles are not complete sentences.
- Titles do not have a period at the end.

Read each paragraph. Circle the best title. Then write the title.

Paragraph 1

_____

My little boy's favorite shoes are his light-up shoes. The shoes are blue and red with Spiderman on them. There are small blue lights in the shoes. He takes a step, and the light flashes. The shoes are a little tight now, but he still wants to wear them every day.

a. My Son Likes Spiderman Shoes.

b. Fun Light-up Shoes

c. Fabulous Blue and Red Light-up Spiderman Shoes for Little Boys

Paragraph 2

_____

My cheap, nylon raincoat is very practical. I can fold it up and put it in my purse. It is very small. I take it with me everywhere. On rainy days, I always have it. It keeps me completely dry. This is important because it often rains, and I usually walk to work.

a. It Is Good to Always Have a Raincoat.

b. My Practical Raincoat

c. Rainy Days at Work

Paragraph 3

_____

In the summer, I always wear my light cotton yellow shirt. I love this shirt because it is very practical in the summer. It has long sleeves. The long sleeves are light, so I do not get too hot.

a. A Yellow Summer Shirt

b. Cotton Clothes are Good for the Summer.

c. A Practical Summer Shirt

Focused Practice

A. *Read the paragraph and answer the questions.*

A Very Useful Apron

My soft cotton apron is a very useful piece of clothing. I love to cook, but I am a messy cook. My apron keeps my clothes clean. It is big, so it covers most of my clothes. It has several pockets. I can put towels and other things in the pockets. It is 15 years old. It is a little old-fashioned, but it is very practical, and I like it a lot.

---

1. What piece of clothing does the paragraph describe? Circle the clothing.

2. What is the topic sentence? Underline it.

3. What is the controlling idea? Circle it.

4. What is the title? Circle it. What does the title tell the reader: Is the paragraph about a favorite or a practical piece of clothing?

5. Are there at least three new vocabulary words or phrases from this unit? Put a star (*) next to them.

B. *Work with a partner. Compare your answers.*

Your Own Writing

Revising Your Draft

A. *Look at your paragraph on page 73. Then read the Revision Checklist and check (✓) your answers. What do you need to revise?*

B. *Revise your paragraph. Add capital letters to the important words in your title.*

Revision Checklist	Yes	No
1. Circle the topic of your paragraph. Are all the sentences about this topic?		
2. Underline the topic sentence. Does it have a controlling idea?		
3. Circle the title of your paragraph. Does it tell the reader about the paragraph?		
4. Did you do the following in your paragraph? • indent the first sentence of the paragraph? • use capital letters and end punctuation?		
5. Put a star (*) next to each new word or phrase from this unit. Are there at least three new words or phrases?		

Step 4 Editing

GRAMMAR PRESENTATION

Before you hand in your paragraph, read it one more time and edit it for errors in grammar. In this editing section, you review the use of *a, an,* and *the.* Think about your paragraph as you review.

A, An, and The

Grammar Notes	Examples
1. Use *a* or *an* (indefinite articles) before a **singular count noun** when you are talking about things in general. Use *a* before a **consonant** sound. Use *an* before a **vowel** sound.	• I want **a suit**. • I don't need **an apron**.

BE CAREFUL! Don't put *a* or *an* before a non-count noun or a plural noun.	• **Wool** is often itchy. (non-count)
	  NOT: A wool is often itchy.
	• I usually wear **jackets**. (plural)
	  NOT: I usually wear a jackets.

2. Use *the* (definite article) for **specific things** that the speaker and listener know about. You can use *the* before **singular count** nouns, **plural count** nouns, and **non-count nouns**.	SALESPERSON: Do you like **the** black suit? CUSTOMER: No, but I like **the** blue suit. • **The** shirt is too small. • **The** shoes are old. • **The** leather is soft.

3. Use *the* when there is only one of something.	• I really like **the** long green **coat**.
	  (*There is only one long green coat in the store.*)
	• **The president** wears baseball caps.
	  (*There is only one president.*)

4. Use *the* when you talk about something for the **second time** and afterwards.	• This store has shorts and T-shirts in my size. **The shorts** are nice. **The T-shirts** are expensive.

Focused Practice

A. *Read the note. Then complete the sentences. Add* a *or* an *when necessary. Remember: Do not use an article before plural or non-count nouns.*

Hello Andy, Daniel, and Sarah,

Here are some hand-me-down clothes from your cousins. They don't fit them. They are too small and tight for them now. They don't need them. I hope you can use them. Here is a list of the clothes.

- 3 dress shirts
- 1 tailored jacket   · 1 apron
- 1 orange T-shirt   · 2 sun hats
- leather boots   · 1 yellow raincoat
- 1 pair of jeans   · 1 casual sport coat
- flip-flops   · 1 everyday dress and 3 formal dresses

Love,

Aunt Diana

Example:

I have _____ dress shirts and __*a*__ tailored jacket for you.

1. There is also _____ orange T-shirt and _____ leather boots.

2. There is _____ pair of jeans.

3. There are _____ flip-flops too.

4. There is _____ apron, _____ sun hats, and _____ raincoat.

5. There is _____ casual sport coat, _____ everyday dress, and _____ formal dresses.

B. *Complete the sentences. Use* a, an, *or* the.

Example:

I need warm clothes. I need __*a*__ wool hat and __*a*__ warm coat.

1. It's cold! You are only wearing a T-shirt! You need _____ warm sweater.

2. It's raining. I need _____ raincoat and _____ umbrella.

3. I want to get my nephew something trendy for his birthday. He wants _____ unusual cap.

4. I don't want _____ cotton mittens. I want _____ wool mittens. They keep my hands warm.

C. *Read the thank you letter to Aunt Diana. Correct six more errors with* **a, an,** *or* **the.**

Dear Aunt Diana,

                   the

Thank you so much for ⌃ clothes. We love them! Andy needed some nice clothes, so he took a tailored jacket and the dress shirts. (I already have a tailored jacket and the dress shirt.) Sarah really likes the dresses. She especially likes an red and yellow everyday dress. I took a leather boots. I also took the jeans and an orange T-shirt.

I am sending you a orange T-shirt too! The T-shirt has my band's name and logo on it. I hope you can come and hear us soon.

Say hello to our cousins!

Sincerely,

Daniel

Your Own Writing

Editing Your Draft

A. *Edit your paragraph for the assignment. Use the Editing Checklist below.*

B. *Write a clean copy of your paragraph. Give it to your teacher.*

Editing Checklist		
Did you . . .	**Yes**	**No**
• use *a*, *an*, and *the* correctly?		
• use new vocabulary from the unit correctly?		
• use a topic sentence with a controlling idea?		
• use complete sentences?		
• include a title?		
• use the correct format, capitalization and punctuation?		

5 Amazing Nature

IN THIS UNIT This unit is about amazing events in nature. What kinds of things happen in nature? What natural events are amazing?

There are many kinds of amazing and unusual natural events. Extreme weather is one kind of natural event. For example, lightning storms are often spectacular. Strong storms with wind and rain or heavy snow are exciting, but sometimes frightening. Rainbows and sunsets, a full moon, and starry skies are also amazing, and they can be very beautiful. Some people spend days looking for these strange or spectacular events. These people "chase" the storms and "follow" the sun.

What natural events do you enjoy seeing?

Planning for Writing

■ BRAINSTORM

A. *Read the questions. Discuss your answers with a partner.*

1. Do you often have extreme weather in your hometown? What is it? What is it like?

2. What are the colors of a rainbow? What are the colors of a sunset? What are the colors of a storm?

3. How do the colors of the rainbow, sunset or storm make you feel?

4. Does one natural event make you feel better than the others?

B. Using a *Wh-* Questions Chart. *A wh- questions chart helps you think about the information you need in your writing. Look at the* wh- *questions chart. Underline the answers in the paragraph below.*

Who was there?	*I* = The writer was there.
What was the event?	There were some amazing thunderstorms.
When was it?	It was in September 2010.
Where was it?	It was in the desert in New Mexico.
How did it look?	It was black and violent. It looked like fire.

Thunderclouds in New Mexico

I saw some amazing thunderstorms in New Mexico in September 2010. I drove across the desert. The sky was clear, but I saw thunderclouds far ahead of me. The thunderclouds were tall and black, and there was lightning inside the clouds. It looked like fire. The storm looked and sounded violent. Under the clouds, the air was black with rain. Luckily, I was far away, so I was safe.

C. *Read the paragraph about snowflakes. Then complete the* wh- *questions chart.*

Watching Snowflakes

I loved walking in the snow and looking at snowflakes in Toronto. In Toronto, snowflakes were the best in January, in the middle of winter. They were all different. Some had six points, and they looked like snowflakes in cartoons. Some looked like stars. Some just looked like frozen drops of water. They always felt soft and light on my tongue! Sometimes I get angry at the snow because it causes bad traffic, and it is uncomfortable. At those times, I try to remember the beautiful snowflake shapes in Toronto. Then I feel calm again.

Who was there?	*I = The writer was there.*
What was the event?	*There were some beautiful* _____ .
When was it?	
Where was it?	
How did it look?	

The Storm Chaser

Tornado Season in Kansas
Snowstorms in Europe Close Airports

1   We read about very bad weather in the news all the time. We often see remarkable photos of weather events. Who takes those photos? And why is that person there?

2   In the United States, Warren Faidley takes many of these photos. Faidley is a professional photographer and storm chaser.

3   Warren took his first famous storm photograph in 1987. He was watching a lightning storm. Lightning hit a gasoline factory. He took a photograph of that exact moment. *Life Magazine* printed the photo. The magazine called Faidley a "storm chaser." That is how his career started.

4   Now Faidley chases storms all the time. He chases tornadoes[1] in the spring. In the summer, he chases lightning storms. In the early fall, he chases hurricanes.[2] In between tornadoes, hurricanes, and lightning storms, Faidley looks for wildfires,[3] hailstorms, snowstorms, or other amazing weather.

5   Faidley also loves taking photographs of rainbows, sunsets, ocean waves, and other beautiful natural events. Often, he just sits quietly in nature. He waits for a beautiful moment to photograph. He feels the beauty of nature, and he tries to put that beauty into a photograph. But we rarely see a newspaper article about a beautiful sunset or a rainbow. So he is not so famous for these things.

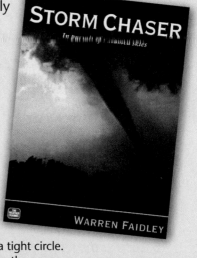

6   Faidley says that he does not like being in danger. He gets into dangerous situations because he wants good photos. He became a bad weather and safety expert because he wanted to stay safe. Now he writes books, helps make movies about storms, and teaches people about safety in dangerous weather.

7   Faidley does many things, but he learned them all because of his first love: photography. Perhaps we should call him "the photograph chaser."

---

[1] **tornado:** a violent storm with strong winds. The winds go around in a tight circle.
[2] **hurricane:** a storm with very strong, fast winds. The storm comes from the ocean.
[3] **wildfires:** fires in a natural, wild area

Building Word Knowledge

Word Partners. There are many kinds of storms. You can use noun + *storm* to describe a specific kind of storm. Here are some examples.

*dust storms: In the Sahara Desert, there are often **dust storms**.*

*rainstorms: **Rainstorms** are common in winter in many places.*

*windstorms: Strong **windstorms** can destroy houses.*

*thunderstorms: **Thunderstorms** always have lightning.*

A. *Look at "The Storm Chaser." Write the names of storms in the article.*

1. _____storm

2. _____storm

3. _____storm

B. *Complete the sentences. Use the correct noun +* storm.

1. Everything was completely white during the _____.

2. Never go out in a _____. The ice can hurt you.

3. A _____ is coming. Bring your umbrella.

4. I left my windows open, and now everything is dirty. There was a

   _____ this morning.

5. I hate the noise in a _____. It scares me.

Comprehension

A. *Read "The Storm Chaser" on page 83 again. Check (✓) the words that describe Warren Faidley.*

_____ storm chaser   _____ weather expert

_____ driver   _____ storm safety expert

_____ photographer   _____ author

_____ factory worker   _____ movie star

B. *Look at the reading again. Then complete the information about Warren Faidley on page 85. Choose the words from the box. Write only the correct words.*

only storms	USA	lightning	The Photograph Chaser
all natural events	Europe	a beautiful sunset	The Storm Chaser

Famous Photographers Today

Name: _Warren Faidley_

Nickname: _____

First famous photo: _____

Country of residence: _____

Likes to take photographs of: _____

C. *Think about the reading. Read the questions and discuss your answers with a partner.*

1. What kinds of photographs do you usually see in newspapers—dangerous weather or quiet natural events? Why do you see a lot of those photographs?

2. How do you think Warren Faidley feels during a storm?

Tip for Writers

Time-Order Words. It may be important to explain the order of events in your writing. You can use the words *before, after,* or *during* + noun to help you.

Before: **Before** *the sunset, the sky was all blue.*

During: **During** *the sunset, we sat on the beach and watched.*

After: **After** *the sunset, it got cold and we went home.*

Read the order of events. Then complete the sentences.

3:00–3:30 P.M. Soraya was outside.

3:30 3:15 P.M. There was a hailstorm. Soraya waited in a store.

3:45 P.M. The hailstorm ended. Soraya walked home.

1. Before the hailstorm, Soraya _was outside_____.

2. During the hailstorm, Soraya _____.

3. After the hailstorm, Soraya _____.

6:00–7:00 P.M. Jacob rushed home.

7:00 P.M.–3:00 A.M. There was a thunderstorm. Jacob stayed awake.

3:00 A.M. Jacob went to sleep.

4. Before the thunderstorm, Jacob _____.

5. During the thunderstorm, Jacob _____.

6. After the thunderstorm, Jacob _____.

Writing a Paragraph

In this unit, you write a paragraph about a natural event. Remember: A paragraph includes a group of sentences about one idea. The first sentence is the topic sentence with a controlling idea. The other sentences in the paragraph are the body sentences. They give information about the controlling idea.

Step 1   Prewriting

Prewriting helps you get ideas and choose your assignment. In this prewriting, you make a *wh-* questions chart. It helps you think about information for the body sentences in your paragraph.

Building Word Knowledge

Vocabulary Log. A vocabulary log helps you keep a record of new vocabulary. Put the words in a vocabulary log into groups of things that are similar in some way. Use a dictionary. Write the meaning of the word and an example sentence. This helps you remember new words better.

Here are some groups for *extreme natural events*.

Land	Sky	Water
earthquake	*eclipse*	*hurricane*
volcano	*meteor*	*glacier*
landslide	*comet*	*waterfall*

A. *Complete the vocabulary log. Use a dictionary to help you.*

▬▬▬ Extreme Natural Events ▬▬▬

Land	Sky	Water
earthquake	*eclipse*	*hurricane*
Meaning: *a sudden shaking of the earth that often causes a lot of damage.*	Meaning: _____	Meaning: _____
Example: *There are often earthquakes in California and Japan.*	Example: _____	Example: _____

B. *Make your own vocabulary log. Add your own word to each group.*

Your Own Writing

Choosing Your Assignment

A. *Choose Assignment 1 or Assignment 2.*

Assignment 1: Describe an amazing weather event you experienced.

Assignment 2: Describe an amazing natural event you experienced (not a weather event).

B. *Read the list of natural events. Some are weather events. Some are other events. Check (✓) the events you know. This will help you choose an event for your assignment.*

Weather Events		Other Events	
☐ rainstorm	☐ dust storm	☐ eclipse	☐ full moon
☐ hailstorm	☐ thunderstorm	☐ earthquake	☐ rainbow
☐ snowstorm	☐ hurricane	☐ volcano	☐ glacier
☐ lightning storm	☐ heat wave	☐ sunset	☐ meteor

C. Checking in. *Share your list of natural events with a partner. Describe the events. Ask your partner questions.*

Example:

Who was there?

What were the events?

How did they look?

D. *Choose one event for your assignment. Write a title at the top of the* wh- *questions chart. Then write complete sentences to answer the questions.*

_____

Who was there?	
What was the event?	
When was it?	
Where was it?	
How did it look?	

■ THE TOPIC SENTENCE

The **topic sentence** in a paragraph gives the **topic** and the **controlling idea**. The topic answers the question *What is the paragraph about?* The controlling idea answers the question *What does the paragraph explain about the topic?*

Examples:

Topic Sentence: I saw a beautiful meteor on a camping trip last summer.

Topic: meteor on a camping trip

Controlling Idea: beautiful

Topic Sentence: In the summer of 1997, I was in a short but frightening lightning storm on Seneca Lake.

Topic: lightning storm on Seneca Lake

Controlling Idea: short but frightening

Topic Sentence: The comet in the August sky was amazing.

Topic: comet

Controlling Idea: amazing

Focused Practice

A. *Circle the topic and underline the controlling idea in each topic sentence.*

Example:

There was a <u>beautiful</u> (rainbow) early yesterday morning.

1. In Yosemite National Park, I saw an amazing waterfall last spring.

2. A few years ago there was a terrible heat wave in Europe.

3. The 1991 Oakland wildfires were frightening.

4. In December 1978, there was a long, very cold snowstorm.

5. The ocean waves last summer were huge and exciting.

B. Writing for the Assignment. *Think about your topic. Write a topic sentence for your assignment. Circle the topic. Underline the controlling idea.*

_____

_____

THE BODY SENTENCES

The topic sentence in a paragraph gives the topic and controlling idea. **Body sentences** explain the topic sentence. All the body sentences support the controlling idea in the topic sentence. They give important information to help the reader understand the idea of the paragraph.

They answer questions such as:

What was the event?

Who was there?

How did it look?

They also give other important information such as:

How did it feel or sound or smell?

Why did it happen?

How did it end?

Focused Practice

A. *Read the topic sentence. Then read the body sentences in the chart. How does each body sentence explain the topic sentence? Complete the chart. Check (✓) the column.*

Topic Sentence: In the summer of 1997, I was in a short but frightening lightning storm on Seneca Lake.

Body Sentences	What was the event?	Who was there?	When was it?	Where was it?	How did it look, feel, sound, or smell?	Why did it happen? How did it end?
1. I was on the lake in a sailboat with my friends.		✓		✓		
2. At first, the weather was beautiful.						
3. But suddenly a strong storm started.						
4. The thunder was loud, and the lightening very bright.						
5. After one hour, the storm stopped, and there was a beautiful rainbow.						
6. The storm damaged the boat, but luckily everyone was OK.						
7. That was an unforgettable summer!						

B. *Read the topic sentence and the body sentences. How does each body sentence explain the topic sentence? Complete the chart. Check (✓) the column. Be careful: Some sentences do not support the topic sentence.*

Topic Sentence: Last spring, my friends visited an amazing waterfall in Yosemite Park.

Body Sentences	What was the event?	Who was there?	When was it?	Where was it?	How did it look, feel, sound, smell?	Why did it happen? How did it end?	This doesn't support the topic sentence.
1. My friends stood at the bottom of the waterfall and looked and listened.							
2. They had backpacks and lunch with them.							
3. The waterfall was very loud.							
4. It sounded like thunder.							
5. I also saw a big thunderstorm last summer.							
6. They felt like the sound was in their body.							
7. The falling water created rainbows at the bottom of the fall.							

C. *Circle the topic. Underline the controlling idea. Then cross out the four sentences that do not support the topic sentence.*

Rainstorms in Singapore

I love the short but powerful rainstorms in Singapore. Before the storms, it is usually warm. Singapore is a large, very clean city in Asia. The air feels heavy and smells like rain. Then the rain begins. The rain feels like a huge bucket of water. It pours down suddenly, and my clothes, hair, and sandals get completely wet, but I do not mind. The rain in Portland, Oregon, is very cold too. That is where I am from. Rain in Singapore always feels good. After the storm, everything smells fresh. The best thing about Singapore is the food!

Building Word Knowledge

Sense Verbs. *Look, feel, taste, smell,* and *sound* are helpful verbs for describing an experience. After these words, you can use an adjective, or *like* + noun. Here are some examples.

Adjective	*Like* **+ Noun**
*The clouds **looked beautiful.***	*The clouds **looked like dancers.***
*The cold rain **felt icy.***	*The cold rain **felt like needles.***
*The snow **tasted light.***	*The snow **tasted like ice.***
*The rain **smelled fresh.***	*The rain **smelled like spring.***
*The thunder **sounded loud.***	*The thunder **sounded like a drum.***

A. *Complete the sentences. Circle the correct adjective or noun. Then write the sentence.*

Example:

The storm sounded like (**frightening** / **a crowd of noisy people**).

The storm sounded like a crowd of noisy people.

1. The ocean smelled (**fishy** / **salt**).

_____

2. The eclipse looked (**colorful** / **an orange ball**).

_____

3. The light rain feels like (**gentle** / **feathers on my skin**).

_____

4. The meteor looked like (**bright** / **a bright line in the sky**).

_____

5. The ocean waves taste (**salty** / **summer**).

_____

6. The volcano looked like (**smoky** / **an explosion in a movie**).

_____

B. *Complete the sentences. Use an adjective or* like + noun.

Example:

Nice sunsets look *like paintings in the sky* _____.

   1. A wildfire smells _____.

   2. Lightning storms sound _____.

   3. The air in a dust storm tastes _____.

   4. A bad rainstorm feels _____.

   5. A full moon looks _____.

C. *Write three sentences about your own topic. Use* look, sound, taste, smell, *or* feel.

   1. _____

   2. _____

   3. _____

Your Own Writing

Finding Out More

A. *Go online. Type the keyword* [the name of your natural event] *or* amazing weather *or* natural phenomena.[1] *Find information about your topic. Find information about another interesting natural event too.*

[1] **phenomena:** (plural) things that happen in nature. The singular form is *phenomenon*.

B. *Write the name of the natural events in the chart. Answer the questions.*

	Event Name _____	**Event Name** _____
When was it?		
Where was it?		
How did it look, feel, taste, smell, or sound?		
Other information:		

C. Checking in. *Share your information about the natural events with a partner. Add ideas you like from your partner's list.*

          ➡

Planning Your Paragraph

A. *Look at the events in your chart. Choose the event for your assignment. You can choose an event from your* wh- *questions chart on page 87, or you can choose from Exercise B on page 92.*

B. Writing for the Assignment. *Look at your topic sentence on page 88, your* wh- *questions chart, and your Finding Out More chart. Use them to help you. Write a paragraph about an experience with amazing weather or another natural event. Give your paragraph a title.*

Example:

The Pink Lake

The Pink Lake is a very special lake in Senegal. I visited the Pink Lake in 1997. It really is pink! The color looks like the fancy soap at my grandmother's house. The water in the lake is very salty. It tastes terrible. The extra salt makes the water pink. At first, it looks very strange, but you get used to it. It is fun to swim in the Pink Lake because your body feels light in very salty water.

Step 3   Revising

Revising your draft makes your writing better. It is an important step in writing. When you revise, you can add and change sentences. You can also add and change words.

Building Word Knowledge

Antonyms. Some pairs of words have opposite meanings. These are antonyms. Learn antonyms together to remember them better. Here are some adjectives that describe natural events. They are antonyms.

violent — peaceful	*frightening — relaxing*	*rough — smooth*
fiery — icy	*wild — calm*	*amazing — ordinary*
colorful — gray	*noisy — quiet*	*strange — normal*

Complete the sentences. Use the antonym of the highlighted words.

Example:

Hurricane Andrew was amazing. Yesterday's rainstorm was _____*ordinary*_____.

1. The sound before the storm was strange, but the sky looked _____.

2. The volcano was fiery. The snow on the mountain was _____.

3. The sunset was colorful. The clouds were _____.

4. A bad snowstorm is frightening. A gentle snowstorm is _____.

5. The waterfall is wild. The lake is _____.

6. Thunder is noisy. A metcor is _____.

7. The tornado felt very violent. The sunset was _____.

8. The waves are rough, but the sand is _____.

Tip for Writers

Idea Connectors. In a paragraph, it is important to connect ideas to each other. **And, but**, and **so** can connect the ideas in sentences to each other. These words help the reader understand the relationship between ideas. Notice the use of the comma.

• *And* prepares the reader for additional information.

There was heavy fog yesterday morning, **and** *it was very cold.*

• *But* prepares the reader for something unexpected.

There was heavy fog yesterday morning, **but** *there were no traffic accidents.*

• *So* prepares the reader for a result.

There was heavy fog yesterday morning, **so** *it was difficult to see.*

B. *Complete the sentences. Use* **and, but,** *or* **so** *to show the relationships in parentheses.*

Example:

There was a dust storm yesterday, ___*and*___ it was very hot. (*additional information*)

1. I swept the floors, _____ my husband dusted everything in the house.

   (*additional information*)

2. I stayed in my office during the storm, _____ my colleague went out.

   (*unexpected*)

3. The storm was over around 5:00 P.M., _____ I went home. (*result*)

4. The windows at my house were open, _____ the house got very dusty.

   (*result*)

5. I closed the windows that morning, _____ the strong wind blew them

   open. (*unexpected*)

C. *Write the topic sentence for your assignment. Add three body sentences. Use* **and, but,** *or* **so.**

Topic Sentence:_____

1. _____

2. _____

3. _____

Focused Practice

A *Read the paragraph and answer the questions.*

> ### A Glacier in Norway
>
> Last year, I visited a beautiful and surprising glacier in Norway. The glacier was icy and white, but the water under the glacier was a beautiful light blue. It looked like a painting of water, not real water. The glacier looked very peaceful and calm from far away, but I walked closer and I had a surprise. The glacier sounded very noisy. It sounded like crashing rocks. I was afraid. I thought, "The glacier is falling!" Then my friend explained the noise. Glaciers usually make sounds because the ice is always moving inside.

1. What is the topic of the paragraph? Circle it.

2. What is the controlling idea? Underline it.

(continued)

Amazing Nature **95**

3. Count the body sentences. How many are there? ____

4. Do all the body sentences support the controlling idea? Check (✓) the

answer. ____ yes ____ no

5. Underline the vocabulary words from this unit. How many are there? ____

B. *Work with a partner. Compare your answers.*

Your Own Writing

Revising Your Draft

A. *Look at your paragraph on page 93. Then read the Revision Checklist and check (✓) your answers. What do you need to revise?*

B. *Revise your paragraph. Remember: Cross out body sentences that do not support the topic sentence.*

Revision Checklist	Yes	No
1. Underline the topic sentence. Is there a clear topic and a controlling idea?		
2. Circle the controlling idea. Does each body sentence explain and support this idea?		
3. Did you do the following in your paragraph? • indent the first sentence of the paragraph?		
• use one space between sentences?		
• use capital letters and correct punctuation?		
• use idea connectors and explain the order of events?		
• give the paragraph a title?		
4. Put a star (*) next to each word or phrase from this unit. Are there at least three new words or phrases?		

■ GRAMMAR PRESENTATION

When writers describe an experience, they often use the simple past tense of verbs. In this editing section, you review the past tense. Before you hand in your paragraph, read it one more time. Edit it for past tense errors.

Simple Past: Regular and Irregular Verbs

Grammar Notes	Examples
1. Use the **simple past** to talk about an event that happened in the past. **Regular verbs** in the simple past **end in -ed**. If the base form ends in **-e**, only add **-d**. If the base form ends in **-y** after a consonant, change the **-y** to **-i**, and add **-ed**. **Irregular verbs** have **different forms** in the simple past. (See the irregular verbs below.) **REMEMBER:** The past forms of **be** are **was** and **were**.	• It **started** to rain. *(start)* • I **arrived** late. *(arrive)* • He **hurried** home. *(hurry)* • The sky **became** dark. *(become)* • We **went** inside. *(go)* • The little girl **was** frightened. *(be)*
2. For a **negative sentence** in the simple past, use **did not** + the **base form** of the verb. Use the contraction **didn't** + the **base form** in conversation and informal writing. **BE CAREFUL!** Don't use **did** or **didn't** with the past tense form of the verb. **REMEMBER:** The negative past forms of **be** are **was not** (**wasn't**) and **were not** (**weren't**).	• He **did not see** the meteor. • He **didn't see** the meteor. NOT: He ~~didn't saw~~ the meteor. • The children **weren't** awake during the storm.

3. Here are some common **irregular verbs** and their simple past forms.

BASE FORM	SIMPLE PAST	BASE FORM	SIMPLE PAST	BASE FORM	SIMPLE PAST
blow	blew	get	got	know	knew
buy	bought	go	went	see	saw
break	broke	grow	grew	sit	sat
come	came	have	had	take	took
feel	felt	hit	hit	think	thought

Amazing Nature   **97**

Focused Practice

A. *Read the sentences. Circle the past tense verb in each sentence.*

1. Warren always liked storms.

2. He grew up in tornado country.

3. He didn't get scared easily.

4. One time, he chased a storm near a river.

5. He was 12 years old.

6. Suddenly, there was a flood.

7. It was dangerous, but Warren felt okay.

8. He didn't stop chasing storms.

B. *Complete the sentences. Use the past tense form of the verb in parentheses.*

1. Warren _____ a regular car to chase storms. (**have**)

2. One time, he _____ in a very bad hailstorm. (**be**)

3. The hail _____ like big white grapefruits. (**look**)

4. The wind _____ very hard. (**blow**)

5. The hail _____ like rocks on the car. (**sound**)

6. The hail _____ the car hard. (**hit**)

7. Hail _____ the windows in his car. (**break**)

8. He _____ frightened. (**be**)

9. He _____ to get a safer car. (**decide**)

10. He _____ a strong truck. (**buy**)

11. He _____ safer in his truck. (**feel**)

C. *Read the paragraph. Correct seven more past tense errors.*

Watching Waves

                      was

The first time I saw the ocean, it ~~is~~ amazing. I was in California. I sit on a wall above the beach for an hour and just watch. I smelled the fresh, salty air. The waves are very violent and strong. At first, they look like big, gentle bumps of water. But then they come close to the sand, and they crashed! The noise is frightening. The water sounds angry. I did not know the ocean was so strong.

Your Own Writing

Editing Your Draft

A. *Edit your paragraph for the assignment. Use the Editing Checklist below.*

B. *Write a clean copy of your paragraph. Give it to your teacher.*

Editing Checklist		
Did you . . .	**Yes**	**No**
• use the simple past of the verbs correctly?		
• use the correct paragraph format?		
• describe an amazing natural event?		
• support the topic sentence with your body sentences?		
• explain the order of events?		
• use correct punctuation and capitalization?		

UNIT 6 Helping Hands

IN THIS UNIT This unit is about helping. When do people need help? What kind of help do people need?

Everyone needs help sometimes. Sick or old people often need help every day. After a natural disaster, many people need help right away. Family members or friends in your community need help from time to time. Fortunately, many people want to help. Some people join organizations to help. Some people travel to other countries. They may help in an international organization, such as the Red Cross. Many helpers do not get paid. These people are called volunteers.

Do you help others? Do people ever help you?

VOLUNTEER

Planning for Writing

▮BRAINSTORM

A. *Read about Doctors Without Borders. Then read the questions. Discuss your answers with a partner.*

Doctors Without Borders

Doctors Without Borders is an organization with about 27,000 volunteers. The volunteers are doctors, nurses, and other helpers from all countries. They give free emergency medical help to people all over the world. It started in France in 1971, and it now helps in 60 countries. The volunteers often work in war or disaster areas. They work in hospitals, give important medicines, feed hungry people, and teach about diseases. Doctors Without Borders believes that all people everywhere must have good medical care.

1. Who are Doctors Without Borders volunteers? What do they do?

2. Do you know any other organizations like this? What do they do?

B. Using a Main Idea / Supporting Details Chart. *This type of chart helps you get ideas for ways to support a topic sentence. Look at the chart below. What supporting details from the chart are in the paragraph in Exercise A? Circle the details in the paragraph.*

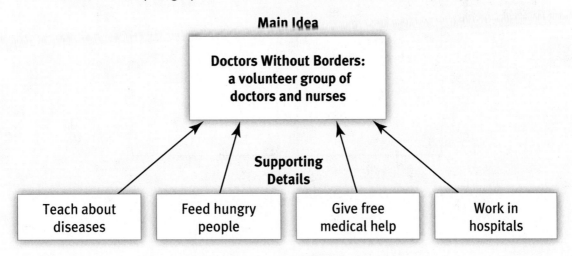

Main Idea

Doctors Without Borders:
a volunteer group of
doctors and nurses

**Supporting
Details**

| Teach about diseases | Feed hungry people | Give free medical help | Work in hospitals |

C. *Read about the Alameda Food Bank. Complete the main idea / supporting details chart with information about the food bank.*

The Alameda Food Bank helps hungry people in Alameda County, California. It has hundreds of volunteers. People and stores donate[1] the food to the food bank. Volunteers organize the food and give it to poor or hungry people. Volunteers help at the food bank because they want everyone in their community to have healthy food.

[1] **donate:** to give something to an organization that needs help

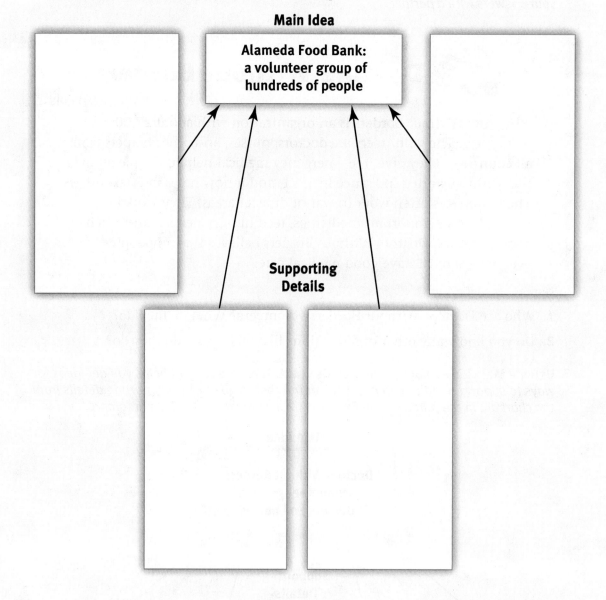

Main Idea

Alameda Food Bank: a volunteer group of hundreds of people

Supporting Details

■ READ

Read the article about the Thorn Tree Project.

The Thorn Tree Project

1　The Thorn Tree Project is not a project about trees at all. It is about schools *under* trees. Chief[1] George Lemerketo, and George and Lucy Leparkiras, started the project in 2001, one year after they met Jane Newman.

2　Jane is a businesswoman from New York City. In 2000, she was on vacation in Kenya. She stopped in a small Sereolipi village in northern Kenya. There she met George Lemerketo, chief of the Sereolipi. Chief George talked to her about the importance of education. The nomadic[2] people of the Sereolipi area did not send their children to school. They moved from place to place with their cattle. The children had to help take care of the animals. The nearest primary schools[3] were often 20 to 40 miles away, so it was impossible for the children to go to school every day. Chief George wanted all nomadic children to go to school. Education helps children. It gives them and their families a better future. He and his friends George Leparkiras, the headmaster of a primary school, and Lucy Leparkiras, the senior teacher at a primary school, had many good ideas. They wanted to help the hundreds of children in northern Kenya go to school, but they needed help too. They needed money for the schools.

3　Jane went home to the United States, but one year later she returned to Kenya. With her help, Chief George and his friends began the Thorn Tree Project. Their goal was to bring as many nomadic children to school as possible. First, they needed to convince parents to send their children to school. So they started several simple preschools near the nomads, under large thorn trees. Little children learned to read and count at the preschools. Their families got excited and decided to send their children to primary school. The number of students in primary schools increased because more families sent their children to school. This is exactly what Chief George, George, and Lucy hoped for, but the children came from far away and needed a place to live. So next, they built more dormitories[4] at the primary schools and bought food for the children to eat. After primary school, the best students want to go to high school,[5] but high school is not free in Kenya. The Thorn Tree Project is very helpful again. It gives scholarships[6] for students to continue their studies.

4　Chief George, George, and Lucy manage the Thorn Tree Project. Jane travels around the world and tells people about the Thorn Tree Project's good work. She asks for donations[7] to help pay for school supplies, food, school uniforms, high school scholarships, teacher training, and more schools. Together these four volunteers help the community help itself. What is their reward? More and more children can go to school. They improve their lives and the lives of their families.

---

[1] **chief:** leader of a group of people
[2] **nomadic:** without a home in one place; moving from place to place
[3] **primary school:** school for children aged approximately 6–13
[4] **dormitories:** buildings for students to live in
[5] **high school:** school for children approximately aged 14–18
[6] **scholarships:** gifts of money to help students go to school
[7] **donations:** things such as money, clothing, and food that people give to help an organization

Building Word Knowledge

Word Families. Word families show the different forms of a word. In this unit, you write about people helping people. *Help* is a verb. *Help* is also a noun. *Helpful* is an adjective. Here are some examples.

Noun	**Verb**	**Adjective**
Chief George needs **help**.	Jane **helps**.	Jane is very **helpful**.
	Jane **helps Chief George**.	
	Jane **helps the chief get** donations.	

A. *Complete the sentences. Use the correct form of* help.

Example:

Anna is a volunteer at the zoo. She is very _____*helpful*_____.

1. She _____ visitors at the zoo.

2. Sometimes small children need _____.

3. Anna lifts them up. She _____ them see the animals.

4. Anna is _____ in other parts of the zoo too.

5. Sometimes the zookeepers need _____.

6. She _____ the zookeepers feed the animals.

7. But she does not _____ in the lion house. That is too dangerous.

B. *Read the ad for a nanny. Complete the sentences with your own ideas.*

Do you need help?

1. I am a professional nanny[1] and I can help _take care of your children_.

2. I can also help you _____.

3. I have a car, so I can help _____.

4. I was a nanny for another family for five years. Their children are older

   now. I helped _____.

If you are interested, call Simone 234-555-0954

---

[1] **nanny:** a person that parents employ to take care of their children

Comprehension

A. *Read "The Thorn Tree Project" on page 103 again. Write T if the statement is true. Write F if the statement is false.*

_____ **1.** Chief George is a kind teacher.

_____ **2.** Before the Thorn Tree Project, most nomadic children in Sereolipi went to preschool.

_____ **3.** The Thorn Tree project helps children in northern Kenya go to school.

_____ **4.** American volunteers teach at the Kenyan schools.

_____ **5.** The Thorn Tree Project is a success.

_____ **6.** The Thorn Tree Project gives money to some children for high school.

B. *Read the article again and look at the chart. Answer the questions.*

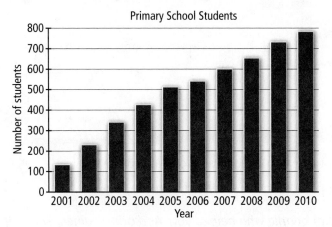

1. Did the number of children in primary schools in northern Kenya increase, decrease, or stay the same after the Thorn Tree Project?

_____

2. How many children were in primary schools in 2001? _____

3. How many children were in primary schools in 2010? _____

4. How does the Thorn Tree Project help children . . .

- at the preschool level? _____

- at the primary level? _____

- at the high school level? _____

C. *Think about the reading. Read the questions and discuss your answers with a partner.*

1. What are reasons people do not send their children to school?

2. How can the Thorn Tree students help their families?

3. How can education help make a better life?

Writing a Paragraph

In this unit, you write a paragraph about helping. Remember: A paragraph includes a group of sentences about one idea. The first sentence is the topic sentence with a controlling idea. The middle sentences are body sentences. They give more information to help the reader understand the topic. A strong paragraph also has a concluding sentence. The concluding sentence tells the reader the paragraph is ending and often repeats the idea in the topic sentence.

Step 1   Prewriting

Prewriting helps you think about and organize ideas for your assignment. In this prewriting, you choose your assignment. Then you make a main idea/supporting details chart.

Your Own Writing

Choosing Your Assignment

A. *Choose Assignment 1 or Assignment 2.*

> **Assignment 1:** Write about a time you helped someone.

> **Assignment 2:** Write about a time someone helped you.

B. *Check (✓) the people you helped or people who helped you. Add other names. This will help you choose the topic for your assignment.*

I helped someone.	Someone helped me.
☐ My older neighbor	☐ My teacher
☐ My classmate	☐ My school
☐ My mother	☐ My family
☐ My friend	☐ My friend
☐ Other: _____	☐ Other: _____

C. Checking in. *Share your list with a partner. Give details about the help. Ask your partner questions and add ideas to your list.*

Examples:

Who did you help? OR Who helped you?

How did you know this person?

Why did you need help? OR Why did the person need your help?

Why did you help? OR Why did the other person help?

What happened?

D. *Complete the main idea/supporting details chart. Choose one person for your assignment. Write the name of the person and the help you gave or received. Then write three supporting details.*

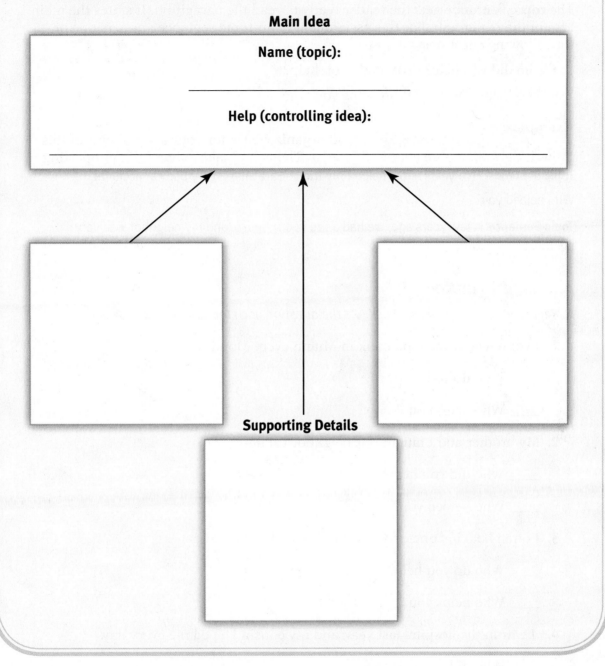

Main Idea

Name (topic):

_____

Help (controlling idea):

_____

Supporting Details

THE TOPIC SENTENCE

The **topic sentence** gets the reader ready to read the paragraph. It states the main idea of the paragraph. For this assignment, your topic sentence answers one of the following questions:

- Who did you help? or Who do you help?
- Who helped you? or Who helps you?

Examples:

Who did you help?

Topic Sentence: Five years ago, I helped my friend Sara after a very bad car accident.

Who helped you?

Topic Sentence: A few years ago, we had a fire in our house, and my neighbor was very helpful.

Focused Practice

A. *Read the topic sentences. Check (✓) the question each topic sentence answers.*

1. I volunteer at the food bank in Miami every Monday.

   _____ Who do you help?

   _____ Who helps you?

2. My brother and I taught our neighbor Chinese.

   _____ Who did you help?

   _____ Who helped you?

3. I often help my uncle fix cars on the weekends.

   _____ Who do you help?

   _____ Who helps you?

4. I was in the hospital last year, and my cousin helped me every day.

   _____ Who did you help?

   _____ Who helped you?

5. My friend's mom needs a lot of help in her store, so I help her on Saturdays.

   _____ Who do you help?

   _____ Who helps you?

B. *Some of the following topic sentences do not answer the questions* Who did you help? *or* Who helped you? *They are not good topic sentences for this assignment. Cross out the sentences that are not good topic sentences for this assignment.*

Example:

~~I have some very old neighbors.~~

1. Last year, I broke my leg, and my best friend was the biggest help.

2. Every weekend, I help my father learn computer skills.

3. Doctors Without Borders is a large organization.

4. My sister helps me do difficult homework.

5. I visited my friends Amy and Jack yesterday.

6. Once a month, I pick up garbage on the beach with the volunteer group Friends of Capitola Beach.

7. I am a volunteer ESL teacher at the Norfolk Adult School.

8. I like to build houses.

C. *Read each topic sentence. Then check (✓) the main idea.*

Example:

Topic Sentence: My dad helps me fix my bike.

___✓___ We work together to repair bikes.

_____ He's a great DIYer.

1. **Topic Sentence:** I broke my arm, and my friend helped me find a doctor.

   _____ He took care of my arm.

   _____ He looked for help with me.

2. **Topic Sentence:** I help coach my daughter's soccer team.

   _____ I like to play soccer.

   _____ I teach soccer.

3. **Topic Sentence:** I often help my grandfather with his computer.

   _____ I help him fix and learn things on the computer.

   _____ Computers are not so difficult to learn.

4. **Topic Sentence:** My friend babysits my children when I am at work.

   _____ She feeds and cares for my daughters during the day.

   _____ She is a really nice person.

5. **Topic Sentence:** My friends and I read to sick children at a local hospital on the weekends.

   _____ We like children a lot, and the hospital is in our neighborhood.

   _____ We volunteer and try to help children feel better.

Your Own Writing

Finding Out More

A. *Go online. Type the keywords* ways to help, ways to help teenagers, ways to help older people, *or* ways to help in [the name of your town]. *Find information about ways people help.*

B. *Answer the questions.*

1. How do people help other people? Write three ways.

_____

_____

_____

2. What types of volunteers are there? Write three types of volunteering.

_____

_____

_____

3. Do you ever help people or volunteer? What do you do?

_____

_____

_____

C. Checking in. *Share your information about helping with a partner. Add ideas and information you like from your partner's answers.*

Planning Your Topic Sentence

A. *Look at your information. Choose the person and help for your assignment. You can choose from your main idea / supporting details chart on page 107, or you can choose ideas from Exercise B above.*

B. Writing for the Assignment. *Think about your topic. Write a topic sentence for your assignment.*

_____

_____

■ BODY SENTENCES

Body sentences give important information to help the reader understand the controlling idea of the paragraph. All the body sentences are about this idea.

Example:

My Brother, Earl

My husband and I help my brother. My brother, Earl, is a very wonderful man, but he has a special disability called Down's Syndrome. Down's Syndrome makes Earl's brain work differently. Because he has this disability, he did not go to regular school, and he does not have a regular job. He lives with us now because he cannot live alone. I drive him to classes at a special center, and I cook for him.

Topic: My brother   **Controlling Idea:** My husband and I help.

Body Sentences 2, 3, 4: Introduce "my brother" and explain why he needs help.

Body Sentences 5, 6: Explain how "my husband and I help my brother."

Focused Practice

Read the topic sentence, the topic, and the controlling idea. Then read the body sentences (a.–h.). Do the body sentences explain who he helps, why he helps, *or* how he helps? *Check (✓) yes or no.*

1. **Topic Sentence:** *I volunteer as a Big Brother for Sammy.*

   Topic: *I volunteer as a Big Brother.*

   Controlling Idea: *Big Brother for Sammy*

   a. Big Brother volunteers are like "big brothers" for teenagers.   ☑ yes ☐ no

   b. I am Sammy's "big brother."   ☐ yes ☐ no

   c. Sammy has no real brothers and sisters.   ☐ yes ☐ no

   d. He has no father, and his mother works until very late every night at her job.   ☐ yes ☐ no

   e. Sammy comes to my apartment most afternoons after school.   ☐ yes ☐ no

   f. Sammy's best friend is Jason.   ☐ yes ☐ no

   g. I used to be a chef in a nice restaurant, but I quit that job.   ☐ yes ☐ no

   h. I help Sammy with his homework.   ☐ yes ☐ no

Do the body sentences explain who they helped, why they helped, or how they helped? Check (✓) yes or no.

2. **Topic Sentence:** *Women in my neighborhood helped with my wedding last year.*

   Topic: *Women in my neighborhood*

   Controlling Idea: *Helped with my wedding*

   a. First, they helped me clean the house. ☐ yes ☐ no

   b. My sister lives in a very nice house in my neighborhood. ☐ yes ☐ no

   c. The house must be very clean because a lot of people come for a wedding! ☐ yes ☐ no

   d. They helped with the laundry and ironing because everyone wants to wear nice clothes for a wedding. ☐ yes ☐ no

   e. You can get very nice clothes at Ali's shop in the town. ☐ yes ☐ no

   f. They helped with cooking too.

   g. I make delicious couscous. ☐ yes ☐ no

   h. I had very good couscous at my aunt's house last night. ☐ yes ☐ no

Tip for Writers

Reasons with *Because*. When you tell a story, it is often helpful to give reasons. Sometimes you need to answer the question "Why?" You can use *because* in your sentences to explain "why." Here are some examples.

The children do not go to school.

Reason: *The school is 20 miles away.*

→ *The children do not go to school **because** the school is 20 miles away.*

You can also write the *because* sentence this way. Notice the use of the comma (,) in this sentence.

→ ***Because** the school is 20 miles away, the children do not go to school.*

A. *Complete the sentences with* because.

1. _____ there was a hurricane, people needed new houses.

2. I volunteered in the Peace Corps _____ I wanted to travel and help people.

3. _____ there was a wildfire, people needed new houses.

4. Many people got sick after the earthquake in Haiti _____ the water was dirty.

B. *Combine the ideas. Write new sentences with* **because.**

Example:

I finished building my house.

Reason: You helped me.

I finished building my house because you helped me.

1. Many small villages have preschools.

   Reason: The Thorn Tree project helped get teachers and school supplies.

   _____

   _____

2. Thousands of people were homeless.

   Reason: The tornado destroyed many houses.

   Because _____

   _____

3. My older neighbor, Mary, needs help shopping.

   Reason: She can't drive.

   Because _____

   _____

4. I passed my Spanish test.

   Reason: Stella helped me study for it.

   Because _____

   _____

Your Own Writing

Planning Your Body Sentences

A. *Look at your topic sentence on page 110, and your main idea/supporting details chart. Think about the answers to these questions to support your topic sentence:*

- Who helped you, or who did you help?
- Why did the person help you, or why did you help the person?
- How did the person help you, or how did you help the person?

B. Writing for the Assignment. *Write your topic sentence. Write five body sentences.*

Topic Sentence:_____

1. _____

_____

2. _____

_____

3. _____

_____

4. _____

_____

5. _____

_____

■ THE CONCLUDING SENTENCE

The **concluding sentence** is the last sentence in the paragraph. It usually repeats similar words or the same words and ideas from the topic sentence. It sometimes gives a personal idea about the topic. It often answers these questions:

- Why was this experience important?

- How did it end?

Example:

My Brother Earl

My husband and I help my brother. My brother, Earl, is a very wonderful man, but he has a special disability called Down's Syndrome. Down's Syndrome makes Earl's brain work differently. Because he has this disability, he did not go to regular school, and he does not have a regular job. He lives with us now because he cannot live alone. I drive him to classes at a special center, and I cook for him. Earl helps me too. **Earl helps me remember the most important thing in life: family.**

In this example the concluding sentence gives a personal idea about the topic and explains why the experience is important.

It repeats the same word in the topic sentence: *help*.

It repeats similar words: *brother → Earl, family*.

Focused Practice

A. *Circle the best concluding sentence for each topic sentence.*

1. **Topic Sentence:** Women in my neighborhood always help with weddings.

    a. Weddings are fun, but they are a lot of work, so we help each other.

    b. I go to a lot of weddings in my neighborhood.

2. **Topic Sentence:** I am a volunteer at the food bank every Saturday.

    a. We usually give food to 150 people in one day.

    b. Volunteering at the food bank helps me remember to be thankful for my own good life.

3. **Topic Sentence:** Last year, a stranger helped me fix the tire on my car.

    a. It took almost an hour, but we fixed it.

    b. Every time I drive my car, I remember the help of a very nice stranger.

4. **Topic Sentence:** I was very sick last month, but luckily my roommate helped me.

    a. I am so lucky to have a kind roommate.

    b. The doctors at the hospital were helpful.

5. **Topic Sentence:** My brother helped me learn to swim.

    a. I was nervous at first, but thanks to my brother I learned to swim.

    b. He told me I need to relax in the water.

B. *Choose the best concluding sentence for each paragraph. Write it in the paragraph.*

Paragraph 1

A Big Brother

I am a Big Brother volunteer. Big Brother volunteers are like "big brothers" for teenagers. I am Sammy's "big brother." Sammy is 15. He has no real brothers or sisters. He has no father, and his mother works until very late every night at her job. Sammy comes to my apartment most afternoons after school. Sometimes we

play a video game or basketball. _____

_____

    a. My own family lives far away, so being Sammy's big brother helps both of us.

    b. He always wants burgers, but I like Chinese food.

    c. Sammy is a really nice kid.

Paragraph 2

Helping Sara

Five years ago, I helped my friend Sara after a very bad car accident. I cooked a lot of food for her every Sunday. I took the food to her house. Sometimes I put food in her freezer so she could eat it later. I also took her three-year-old daughter to the park sometimes. _____

_____

    a. I am glad I helped her because she is a very good friend.

    b. Sara's favorite food is chicken and rice.

    c. It was important to cook really healthy food.

Paragraph 3

A Song Writing Partner

My good friend Steve helps me write songs. He is a really good helper. He gives me a lot of ideas for new tunes or for new words. Sometimes he does not like a song, and we argue. But then a new idea comes, and the song is better.

_____

_____

    a. Writing good songs is hard work, but Steve is a good partner.

    b. My favorite kind of music is rock.

    c. Steve helps me write songs.

Paragraph 4

A Tough Basketball Teacher

My uncle helps me practice basketball. He is a very good basketball player. He played on his college team. He gives me tips. He makes me do the same things over and over until I do them right. He is a tough teacher, but he is good.

_____

_____

    a. I play basketball really well now and make my uncle proud.

    b. We practice every Monday and Wednesday evening.

    c. He helps me learn baseball as well.

Your Own Writing

Planning Your Concluding Sentence

A. *Look at your topic sentence and body sentences on page 114. Answer the questions.*

What is the topic?

_____

What is the controlling idea?

_____

What is your personal idea about the topic?

_____

Why was this experience important?

_____

How did it end?

_____

B. *Write a concluding sentence for your paragraph.*

_____

_____

C. Writing for the Assignment. *Write a paragraph about a time when you helped someone or someone helped you. Use your topic sentence, body sentences, and concluding sentence. Give your paragraph a title.*

_____

_____

_____

_____

_____

_____

_____

Step 3 Revising

Revising your draft is another important step. Revising makes your writing better. When you revise you can add new information or facts, or you can make your writing clearer.

Building Word Knowledge

Suffix -*ful*. Adjectives are useful for describing people or things. You can sometimes make an adjective by adding *-ful* to the end of a noun or a verb. *-ful* is a suffix. It means "full of" or "a lot." For example, *helpful* means *full of help* or *helps a lot*. Here are some other examples.

thank — thankful   beauty — beautiful

thought — thoughtful   forget — forgetful

use — useful   power — powerful

pain — painful   success — successful

A. *Complete the sentences. Use the adjective of the highlighted words.*

Example:

Thank you for your help. You are very _____*helpful*_____ .

  1. My mom has a lot of success in her job. She is _____ .

  2. Sara said "Thank you" many times. She was _____ .

  3. Roberto has pain in his back. His back is _____ .

  4. That house is a beauty! It is very _____ .

  5. Mrs. Morse forgets things often. She is a _____ person.

  6. The president has a lot of power. He is _____ .

B. *Complete these sentences. Use an adjective with* -ful.

  1. Thank you for bringing me dinner! You are very _____ .

  2. The students are _____ for the Thorn Tree scholarships.

  3. I broke my arm last year. It was very _____ for about a week.

  4. I always visit Grandma on Saturdays. Sometimes she is surprised to see me.

     She is _____ these days.

5. I help children learn to paint after school. Look at the _____

paintings they made.

6. Emmet swept the house and did the laundry. He was very _____

today!

C. *Write three sentences for your assignment. Use three adjectives with* -ful.

1. _____

2. _____

3. _____

Tip for Writers

By + Verb *-ing.* When you write about helping, sometimes you need to answer the question *How did you help?* To explain *how,* you can use *by* + a verb with *-ing* on the end. Here are some examples.

I help my neighbor **by going** *to the store for her.*

My dad helps me **by taking** *care of my children.*

The Thorn Tree Project helps schools **by building** *dormitories.*

A. *Underline the words in the sentence that answer the question* How?

Example:

The project helps good students <u>by giving them scholarships</u>.

1. Doctors Without Borders helps people by sending doctors to places without doctors.

2. David does not have time to volunteer, but he helps Amnesty International by sending money.

3. Míguel helps at his children's school by organizing games at lunchtime.

4. Job Tech Skills Central helps people without jobs by teaching them to use and fix computers.

B. *Write two sentences and answer the question* How did you help? *or* How did someone help you? *Use* by + *a verb with* -ing.

1. _____

   _____

   _____

2. _____

   _____

   _____

Focused Practice

A. *Read the paragraph and answer the questions.*

Helping with Babies

I help my aunt take care of her new babies. Aunt Asme had triplets last month, so now she has three beautiful new babies. She cannot take care of them herself because it is too much work. Sometimes I get up at night with the babies and feed them. I drive my aunt and the babies to the doctor. Asme is very thankful for my help, and I am happy to help. I love babies, and I think helping family members is important.

---

1. Who did the writer help? Circle the name.

2. What is the topic sentence? Underline it.

3. Count the body sentences. How many are there? _____

4. Do all the body sentences support the topic sentence? Check (✓) the answer.
   _____ yes _____ no

5. Is there a concluding sentence? Circle it.

6. Does the concluding sentence answer at least one of these questions? Check (✓) the questions.

   ☐ Why was this experience important?

   ☐ How did it end?

B. *Work with a partner. Compare your answers*

Your Own Writing

Revising Your Draft

A. *Look at your paragraph on page 117. Then read the Revision Checklist and check (✓) your answers. What do you need to revise?*

B. *Revise your paragraph. When possible, add sentences with* by + *a verb with* -ing *to explain* how, *and adjectives with the suffix* -ful.

Revision Checklist	Yes	No
1. Underline the topic sentence. Is the paragraph about helping?		
2. Do the body sentences answer these questions?		
• Who helped?		
• Why did the person help?		
• How did the person help?		
3. Underline the concluding sentence. Does the concluding sentence answer one of these questions?		
• Why was this experience important?		
• How did it end?		
• What is the personal idea about the topic?		
4. Put a star (*) next to each new word from this unit. Are there at least three new words?		

■ GRAMMAR PRESENTATION

Before you hand in your paragraph, read it one more time, and edit it for errors. In this editing section, you review subject and object pronouns. Think about your paragraph as you review.

Subject and Object Pronouns

Grammar Notes	Examples
1. *I*, *you*, *he*, *she*, *it*, *we*, and *they* are **subject pronouns**. They replace a subject noun.	• **The boys** need help with their homework. **They** can't understand the directions.
2. *Me*, *you*, *him*, *her*, *it*, *us*, and *them* are **object pronouns**. They replace an object noun. Object pronouns often come **after prepositions** such as *to* or *for*. Note: Sentences can have more than one object.	subject / object noun / noun • Jamal helps **Mrs. Ng.** subject / object pronoun / pronoun • He helps **her.** • She doesn't give money **to him.** • He buys groceries **for her.** • He buys **them for her.**
3. *You* and *it* are both subject and object pronouns.	subject ... object • **You**'re a volunteer. They don't pay **you.** subject ... object • **It**'s a good organization. I like **it.**
4. The pronoun *you* is the same for singular and plural. When *you* is plural, we sometimes add the word *both* to make the sentence clearer.	• I can help **you.** (*you* = Pauline) • Can **you** help me? (*you* = you and Tomiko) • Can **you both** help me?

Focused Practice

A. *Underline the subject noun and object noun in each sentence. Write* S *above the subject. Write* O *above the object. Notice that some sentences have more than one object.*

Example:

   S   O
<u>Dr. Ziad</u> helps <u>sick children</u>.

1. Zoe and I bought food.

2. Zoe and I bought food for our neighbor, José.

3. Sun Mee and Maria always bring the mail to Mr. Rodriguez.

4. John helped the boys after school.

B. *Read the sentences in Exercise A. Write each sentence with subject pronouns and object pronouns. Notice some sentences have more than one object pronoun.*

Example:

Dr. Ziad helps sick children.

He helps them.

1. _____

2. _____

3. _____

4. _____

C. *Read the paragraph. Correct five more subject pronoun and object pronoun errors.*

> They
> I help my uncle and aunt with their computer. He do not understand
> computers. I understand them well. My uncle needs help with Facebook and email.
> She likes to stay in touch with family on email and Facebook. My aunt is an artist.
> She has a website for her art. They often wants to add new paintings to her website.
> Sometimes I teach my aunt and uncle to do things themselves. Sometimes I just do
> things for her. I like helping they. They are always thankful for my help. I often learn
> new things when I am helping us.

Your Own Writing

Editing Your Draft

A. *Edit your paragraph for the assignment. Use the Editing Checklist below.*

B. *Write a clean copy of your paragraph. Give it to your teacher.*

Editing Checklist		
Did you . . .	**Yes**	**No**
• use subject and object pronouns correctly?		
• use vocabulary from the unit correctly?		
• use the correct paragraph format?		

7 Home Sweet Home

IN THIS UNIT   This unit is about things that make you feel at home. How can people feel at home in places like school or an office?

What makes people feel at home? "Home" is the place where you are the most comfortable. Some people spend a lot of time away from their home, for example at work or at school, so they often do things to make themselves feel at home. Some people put photos on their walls. Some people need to have their favorite music with them. Others need to make a space very colorful.

Where do you feel at home? Why do you feel at home there?

"Home sweet home"

Planning for Writing

▪ BRAINSTORM

A. *Look at the photos. What things make this bedroom homey? What makes the office homey? Check (✓) your answers in the charts. Then compare your answers with a partner.*

The Bedroom	
pictures	☐
bright colors	☐
plants	☐
books	☐
a computer	☐
sports equipment	☐
musical instruments	☐
special furniture	☐
other: _____	

The Office	
pictures	☐
bright colors	☐
plants	☐
books	☐
a computer	☐
sports equipment	☐
musical instruments	☐
special furniture	☐
other: _____	

B. *Draw objects in this room that make you feel at home and label them. Use ideas from Exercise A on page 125 or use your own ideas. Then discuss with a partner. Why do these items make this space feel like home?*

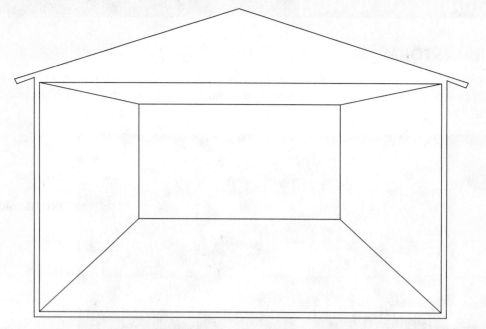

C. **Using an E-chart.** *An E-chart helps you think of reasons and examples for your writing. Look at the E-chart below. Then look at the bedroom on page 125. What makes it feel homey? Read the Reasons and Examples below. Choose the object from the bedroom that belongs in the E-chart. Write it in the chart.*

	Reasons and Examples
The Object	love music
	favorite past time is playing the guitar
	reminds me of my best friends in my band

D. *Make an E-chart for one of the objects in your drawing in Exercise B. Write three reasons or examples that show why the object makes the room homey. Work with a partner. Compare your ideas.*

	Reasons and Examples
The Object	

Read the article about a neighborhood in New Orleans.

New Houses for the Lower Ninth Ward

1   The Lower Ninth Ward is a neighborhood in New Orleans. It was never a fancy neighborhood, but it was friendly. People knew each other. They lived there for a long time. Some people grew up there. People felt at home in the Lower Ninth Ward.

2   In 2005, Hurricane Katrina destroyed the Lower Ninth Ward. It was a terrible time. All the residents[1] became homeless. They had to find other places to stay. Some stayed with family in other cities. Some stayed in emergency housing. Help came very slowly.

3   People from the Lower Ninth Ward were homesick for their neighborhood. They asked, "Is anyone going to rebuild the Lower Ninth Ward?" After a few months, an unlikely person began talking to residents and answering this question.

4   Brad Pitt loves New Orleans. He was very upset when he saw the destruction[2] there, especially in the Lower Ninth Ward. Pitt is a famous actor, but he has another interest too: architecture.[3] Pitt and some architect[4] friends talked to Lower Ninth Ward residents about houses. One elderly man missed his neighborhood badly. He said to Pitt, "Help make it right." So Brad Pitt started the Make It Right organization.

5   The Make It Right organization is building 150 new houses in the Lower Ninth Ward. The architects thought carefully about what people in that neighborhood needed. They thought about the cost, the environment and weather, and the community. So they made the houses inexpensive

Traditional New Orleans house

to build. All the houses are "green"[5], so they use less energy than other houses. They are all high off the ground. That way they are safe when floods happen. One style of Make It Right house can float[6] like a boat in a really big flood.

6   The Make It Right houses will stay cool in hot New Orleans summers. Most houses have front porches because people in New Orleans often sit outside on warm evenings. One kind of house has tall plants on one side. The plants keep the house cool.

7   A few people in New Orleans are not happy with these brightly-colored houses. Some architects and some residents from other parts of the city say, "These houses do not look right in the traditional city of New Orleans. They look very different from traditional New Orleans houses." But most people from the Lower Ninth Ward are grateful to Make It Right for the houses. They want to return to their neighborhood and rebuild their community. They want their children to play outside. They want to share iced tea and conversation on their front porches again. They are eager[7] to make their new modern houses into comfortable homes.

---

[1] **residents:** people who live in a certain place
[2] **destruction:** destroyed area
[3] **architecture:** the design of a building
[4] **architect:** a person who designs buildings
[5] **green:** good for the environment
[6] **float:** to stay on top of water
[7] **eager:** wanting to do something very much

Make It Right house

Building Word Knowledge

Expressions with *Home*. In English, *home* means a place where you live and feel comfortable, especially with your family and friends. There are many expressions and words with *home*. Learn these expressions. They can help you with your assignment. Here are some examples.

feel at home	*homeless*
away from home	*homesick*
homey	*make yourself (myself, etc.) at home*
make your (my, etc.) house a home	

A. *Work in a group. Match the words and expressions with the definitions. Use your dictionary and look for the word* **home** *to help you.*

1. feel at home	_____ **a.** comfortable and pleasant, like home
2. away from home	_1_ **b.** be happy and comfortable somewhere
3. homey	_____ **c.** not home
4. make your house a home	_____ **d.** without a place to live
5. homeless	_____ **e.** sad because you are away from your home
6. homesick	_____ **f.** create a comfortable place for yourself
7. make yourself at home	_____ **g.** a nice thing to say to a house guest

B. *Complete the sentences. Use a word or expression with* **home**.

Example:

Welcome! Come in! Relax! _____Make yourself at home_____.

1. Joey lost his house in the fire. Now he is _____.

2. I use my phone to video chat with my children. I am

   _____ several days a week.

3. I have a nice apartment, but I don't know my roommates very well. I don't

   _____ there.

4. I had a terrible time. I missed my family. I was very

   _____.

5. I moved into a new house last week. I put all of my family photos on the

walls. Those photos _____.

6. My uncle's house is very comfortable, and it always smells like fresh bread.

His house is very _____.

C. *Answer the questions and discuss with a partner.*

1. Where do you feel at home?

2. When do you get homesick?

3. At whose house can you make yourself at home?

Comprehension

A. *Read "New Houses for the Lower Ninth Ward" on page 127 again. Circle the answers.*

1. What is the main idea of the article?

    a. The Lower Ninth Ward is getting modern, green houses from the Make It Right organization.

    b. Brad Pitt is a famous actor, but he is also interested in green architecture.

    c. Many people do not like the new houses because they do not make New Orleans traditional.

2. What is the conclusion of the article?

    a. The Make It Right houses are not very popular.

    b. The Lower Ninth Ward is a strong community again.

    c. People hope the Make It Right houses can rebuild their community.

B. *Think about the reading. Read the questions and discuss your answers with a partner.*

1. How do some Make It Right houses stay cool? How do other houses stay cool in the summer?

2. How are Lower Ninth Ward residents rebuilding their community? How can they make their neighborhood comfortable again?

3. Do you feel more comfortable in a traditional style house or a modern one? Explain your answer.

Writing an Opinion Paragraph

In this unit, you write a paragraph about making yourself feel at home. In this paragraph, first you give your own idea, your opinion. Then you give reasons and examples. Remember: A paragraph has a topic sentence with one controlling idea. All the body sentences help the reader understand the idea. The concluding sentence ends the paragraph. It summarizes or gives a personal idea.

Step 1   Prewriting

In this prewriting, you choose your assignment. Then you make an E-chart. The E-chart helps you write your opinion and support your opinion with examples.

Building Word Knowledge

Make. *Make* is a verb. Use *make* + a noun or object pronoun + adjective to describe what causes people to feel a certain way. Use it to describe what causes things to be a certain way too. Here are some examples.

*These houses **make us happy**.*   *Big windows **make a room bright**.*

*Make It Right **makes people thankful**.*   *Flowers **make my office homey**.*

A. *Complete the sentences. Use the words in the box.*

angry	big	colorful	happy	modern	~~new~~

Example: Brad Pitt wants to make the neighborhood _____*new*_____ again.

1. I love music. Music makes me _____.

2. Let's make the house _____. I have red, orange, and

   purple paint.

3. My noisy, rude neighbor makes me _____.

4. This porch is small. Let's make it _____.

5. This kitchen feels old. How can we make it _____?

B. *Complete the sentences. Use your own ideas.*

1. _____ makes me happy at home.

2. _____ makes people comfortable at work.

3. _____ makes me relaxed at school.

Your Own Writing

Choosing Your Assignment

A. *Choose Assignment 1 or Assignment 2.*

Assignment 1: Describe what makes your house or apartment a home.

Assignment 2: Describe what makes your space away from home feel homey.

B. *Check (✓) the things that help you feel at home. Add your own ideas. This will help you choose the topic for your assignment.*

These things . . .		make my house a home.	make my space away from home feel homey.
Decorations	posters	☐	☐
	paintings	☐	☐
	_____	☐	☐
Furniture	comfortable chair	☐	☐
	sofa	☐	☐
	_____	☐	☐
Souvenirs	postcards	☐	☐
	_____	☐	☐
Hobbies	basketball	☐	☐
	guitar	☐	☐
	_____	☐	☐
Electronic devices	TV	☐	☐
	computer	☐	☐
	_____	☐	☐
Handmade things	quilt	☐	☐
	table	☐	☐
	_____	☐	☐
Photos	of family	☐	☐
	of places	☐	☐
	_____	☐	☐
Other things	plants	☐	☐
	books	☐	☐
	_____	☐	☐

➡

C. Checking in. *Share your list with a partner. Discuss your ideas. Ask your partner questions.*

Examples:

What things make you feel at home?

Why are they important to you?

How do they make you feel?

What do they look like?

D. *Choose one item for your assignment. Complete the E-chart. Write the item on the left side of your E-chart. Then complete the chart with three reasons or examples.*

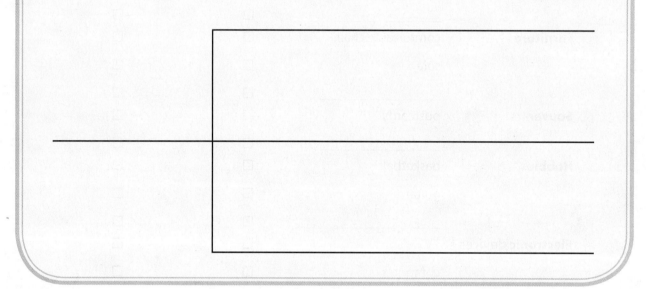

Step 2   Writing the First Draft

■ THE TOPIC SENTENCE

The topic sentence tells the reader what the paragraph is about. In this assignment, your topic sentence introduces your opinion about something that makes you feel at home. An **opinion** tells your idea or feeling about something. An opinion is not a **fact**. You can prove or measure a fact. You cannot prove or measure an opinion. An opinion is your own view.

Example:

An opinion: The large painting of my grandparents' house makes my apartment a home for me.

A fact: I have a large painting of my grandparent's house.

Focused Practice

A. *Read the sentences. Check (✓) the opinions.*

Example:

_____ **a.** I travel a lot for business and stay at hotels.

__✓__ **b.** I love the smell of coffee in my hotel room because it makes me feel at home.

1.

_____ **a.** Fresh flowers make my office feel homey.

_____ **b.** My husband buys me fresh flowers every Monday for my office.

2.

_____ **a.** Seven hundred students live in the dormitories at my university.

_____ **b.** I added my large chair and rug from my parents' house, and now my dorm room feels like home.

3.

_____ **a.** I love living in the country with lots of trees around me because it smells like home to me.

_____ **b.** My small town is in the country, about a two-hour drive from Little Rock, with lots of trees around it.

4.

_____ **a.** My cell phone helps me feel at home everywhere.

_____ **b.** My friends and I call each other many times every day.

B. *Read each paragraph. Underline the topic sentence. Check (✓) the opinion in the topic sentence.*

Paragraph 1

My Turkish Rug

My Turkish rug makes my house a home. I bought this rug in Turkey about 15 years ago. I love its beautiful colors: green, dark red, and yellow. The rug makes me feel warm in any new house or apartment. I remember my trip to Turkey and all of my other trips to interesting places when I look at that rug.

_____ **a.** My rug makes my house homey.

_____ **b.** I love Turkey.

_____ **c.** The rug is colorful.

Paragraph 2

Driving

I feel less homesick when I have my son's artwork with me on trips. I am a truck driver, and I am away from home a lot. My son's artwork makes me happy. I look at it and think of him. It helps me remember the reason I work so hard.

_____ **a.** I don't like traveling.

_____ **b.** My son's artwork makes me less homesick.

_____ **c.** I am away from home a lot.

C. *Read each paragraph. Check (✓) the best topic sentence for each paragraph. Then write the topic sentence in the paragraph.*

Paragraph 1

_____

I have a lovely light brown blanket on my bed. Three white pillows are on top of the bed. The bedroom floor and furniture are light brown wood. The walls are very light brown. Neutral colors are quiet. They help me relax.

_____ **a.** I feel at home with my light brown blanket.

_____ **b.** I have a large bed in my room.

_____ **c.** Soft, neutral colors make me feel comfortable in my room.

Paragraph 2

_____

I have a small vegetable garden in one corner. There are three rosebushes near the fence. There is a small pond with fish in the middle of my garden. When I have a stressful day, I go home and sit in my garden.

_____ **a.** Plants make me feel at home in my house.

_____ **b.** My garden is the most homey and relaxing place in the world.

_____ **c.** There are many vegetables in my garden, and you will like them.

Your Own Writing

Finding Out More

A. *Go online. Type the keywords* homey office, images *for* homey dorm room, cozy spaces, cozy rooms, *or* images for [name of your own item]. *Find pictures of things that make you feel at home.*

B. *Write the keywords in the chart. Answer the question.*

Keywords	What makes the images homey?

C. Checking in. *Share your information about the images with a partner. Add information you like from your partner's chart.*

Planning Your Topic Sentence

A. *Look at your information in the chart. Choose the item for your assignment. You can choose the item in your E-chart on page 132, or you can choose an item from your chart in Exercise B above.*

B. Writing for the Assignment. *Think about your topic. Write a topic sentence for your assignment.*

_____

_____

■ BODY SENTENCES

Body sentences help the reader understand the topic sentence. For an opinion paragraph, body sentences give **reasons** and **examples**. The reasons and examples help the reader understand the writer's opinion.

Example:

Feeling at Home in Other Places

<u>I like to have things I made myself around me.</u> They make me feel at home when I am away from home. For example, I lived at my aunt's house last year, and I put some of my drawings on the wall. Now I have an apartment with four other people. Right now, I am building a table. My apartment will feel cozier with my handmade table.

Opinion (topic sentence): I like to have things I made myself around me.

Reason: They make me feel at home when I am away from home.

Examples of "things I made myself": my drawings, a table

Focused Practice

Read the paragraphs. Underline the opinion (topic sentence). Check (✓) the reasons and examples that help the reader understand the opinion.

Paragraph 1

Remembering to Laugh at Work

Interesting, funny things in my office make me feel comfortable at work. For example, I have comics and jokes on my wall. There are some toys on my desk. I have a tiny robot. All these things remind me to laugh, and laughing helps me relax at work.

Reasons they "make me feel comfortable":

_____ They make me laugh at work.

_____ They remind me of home.

_____ They make me relax.

Examples of "funny things in my office":

_____ comics and jokes

_____ toys

_____ a tiny robot

_____ desk

_____ walls

Paragraph 2

The Comfy Chair

My comfortable chair makes my living room cozy. It's a big, old, soft chair. I sit there with my cat and watch TV in the evenings. I often bring a blanket to my chair and I read. Sometimes I even fall asleep there. Visitors always choose that chair to sit in. Everyone loves my big, old living room chair.

Reasons my chair "makes my living room cozy":

_____ It's big, old, and soft.

_____ Visitors choose it.

_____ I sit in it in the evenings.

Examples of cozy things to do in my comfortable chair:

_____ watch TV

_____ invite people

_____ fall asleep

_____ sit

_____ read

Paragraph 3

Making an Office Cheerful

My office has no windows, so I bring things to my office to make it bright and cheerful. For instance, I put a colorful poster on the wall. I bought a red flower vase, so now I can have fresh flowers on my desk. It makes it easy for me to work in a cheerful office.

Reasons "I bring things to my office":

_____ It makes it easy to work in a cheerful office.

_____ I like to work in an office.

_____ There are no windows.

Examples of things that make my office bright and cheerful:

_____ windows

_____ colorful poster

_____ wall

_____ red flower vase

_____ fresh flowers

_____ work

Tip for Writers

Introducing Examples. Use *for instance* or *for example* to introduce examples in a paragraph. Always use a comma after these phrases. Here are some examples.

- *Interesting, funny things in my office make me feel comfortable at work.* **For example,** *I have comics and jokes on my wall.*

- *My office has no windows, so I bring things to my office and make it bright and cheerful.* **For instance,** *I put a colorful poster on the wall.*

A. *Complete the sentences. Add* For example *or* For instance. *Some sentences are not examples. Do not add phrases to those sentences.*

Example:

Many musical instruments make my house homey. For example, I have an electric guitar in my living room.

1. I love my computer for many reasons. It helps me stay in touch with friends.

2. I always take a few things from home on business trips so that I don't feel homesick. I bring a photo of my family.

3. I painted my room bright purple. Then I made some green curtains for the windows.

4. Books always make a house a home for me. I always bring my favorite book of poems with me to a new place.

5. We need to make this house homey. We also need to meet our neighbors.

B. *Complete the sentences. Use your own ideas.*

1. There are many things that help me feel at home in my apartment. For example, _____

_____.

2. Teenagers often decorate their rooms in very interesting ways. For instance,

_____

_____.

3. There are many places I feel at home. For example, _____

_____

_____.

Your Own Writing

Planning Your Body Sentences

A. *Look at your topic sentence on page 135. List reasons and examples below to explain your topic sentence. Use your E-chart to help you.*

Reasons

_____

_____

_____

Examples

_____

_____

_____

B. Writing for the Assignment. *Write your topic sentence. Write five body sentences. Include reasons and examples in your sentences.*

Topic Sentence: _____

_____

1. _____

_____

2. _____

_____

3. _____

_____

4. _____

_____

5. _____

_____

■ THE CONCLUDING SENTENCE

The **concluding sentence** ends the paragraph. Remember: It usually repeats similar words and ideas from the topic sentence. For this assignment, the concluding sentence might

- tell your hope or idea for the future.
- summarize the paragraph.
- add one final opinion to the topic sentence.

Example:

> ### My Guitar, My Friend
>
> My guitar makes me feel at home in new places. Playing the guitar helps me relax. It also helps me make friends in new places. A lot of people like to sing together. They do not have to speak the same language. Often, here in the United States, I play songs from my country, and I feel less homesick.

Possible Concluding Sentences:

An idea about the future: *With my guitar, I will always feel at home away from home.*

A summary: *My guitar helps me in so many ways.*

A final opinion: *My guitar is like a good friend.*

Focused Practice

Read the topic sentence. Cross out the one sentence that is not a good concluding sentence.

Example:

Topic Sentence: I like to have a party in my house to make a house a home.

a. Friends make a house a home.

b. A party with friends makes my house feel homey.

c. ~~I'm going to have a birthday party soon.~~

1. **Topic Sentence:** Photos of my family make me happy when I am away from home.

   a. I have one photo of my sister with me at a swimming pool in 1983.

   b. When I am away from my family, my photos make me feel close to them.

   c. My family photos are comforting.

2. **Topic Sentence:** My house is a home when I have a piano.

    a. I hope I can always have a piano in my home.

    b. I will always have a piano because playing music makes me happy.

    c. I want to teach piano lessons.

3. **Topic Sentence:** I think green plants make any place a home.

    a. I need live, green plants to feel comfortable.

    b. There is a nice park near my apartment.

    c. I hope that I never live in a place without plants.

Your Own Writing

Planning Your Concluding Sentence

A. *Look at your topic sentence and body sentences on page 139. Answer the questions.*

What is your idea about the future?

_____

What is a summary of your opinion?

_____

What is one additional opinion about your topic sentence?

_____

B. *Write a concluding sentence for your paragraph.*

_____

C. Writing for the Assignment. *Write a paragraph about what makes you feel at home or what makes a space homey for you. Use your topic sentence, body sentences, and concluding sentence. Give your paragraph a title.*

_____

_____

_____

_____

_____

Revising your draft makes your writing better. Revising means changing sentences, words, or ideas. When you revise, you try to make your writing clearer for your reader.

Tip for Writers

Reasons and Examples. When you write about your opinion, you need to include reasons and examples. Reasons and examples help explain your opinion. When the reasons and examples do not explain your opinion, they are not helpful to the reader. Remove irrelevant (not helpful) reasons and examples from your paragraph.

A. *Read each topic sentence. Circle the two reasons or examples that explain the opinion in the topic sentence.*

Example:

Topic Sentence: I think a lot of soccer posters, magazines, and sports equipment make a room comfortable.

a. For example, Pele was a really famous Brazilian soccer player, so I want to meet him.

(b.) For instance, I love reading about my favorite soccer players, so my room is full of sports magazines.

(c.) For example, I have a lot of equipment in my room because I love playing soccer.

1. **Topic Sentence:** I think my favorite books make my living room homey.

   a. I lie on the couch and read all the time.

   b. Books make me feel comfortable.

   c. My couch is an important part of my living room too.

2. **Topic Sentence:** I always carry a photo of my brother and me from 1989.

   a. My brother and I travelled together that year.

   b. The photo brings back memories of our travels.

   c. My brother is an engineer now.

3. **Topic Sentence**: Photos on a fridge always make a kitchen homey.

   a. For instance, the calendar on my refrigerator organizes my days.

   b. For example, the picture of my hometown in Guatemala makes me feel at home.

   c. For instance, the photo of my husband makes me happy.

B. *Read the paragraphs. Cross out the irrelevant examples or reasons.*

Paragraph 1

Droopy

Droopy is a very old stuffed animal, but he makes my bedroom cozy and safe. Droopy is a dog. I got Droopy when I was two years old. He kept me safe at night, so I slept with him for many years. He is not a real dog, but he still makes me feel safe. He also reminds me of many happy times when I was a child. My room was small, but it had a big window with lots of light. Now, Droopy stays in a small basket on a shelf. He is very old and ragged, but he is full of memories.

Paragraph 2

Colorful Things

Colorful things make me feel comfortable in unfamiliar places. At home, my walls were all different colors: green, red, and orange. In my apartment now, I cannot paint the white walls, so I find other ways to add color. Sometimes I put a piece of colorful cloth on the wall. Last year, I did not have cloth, so I used yellow and orange paper on one wall in my room. Two years ago, I hung some of my favorite colorful shirts and scarves on my wall. Adding color is not difficult or expensive, and it makes me happy. Also, I have some beautiful scarves that I bought in my hometown.

Focused Practice

A. *Read the paragraph and answer the questions.*

Home Sweet Home

The "Home Sweet Home" sign in my apartment helps me feel less homesick. I moved to Texas to go to college last year. I did not bring many things with me, but I needed the "Home Sweet Home" sign. My grandmother made it. She sewed it with brightly colored thread. The sign makes me happy. It reminds me of my grandmother and grandfather and our family farm. When I read "Home Sweet Home," I smile and I think about home.

---

1. What makes the author feel at home? Circle the item.

2. Why is the item important? Underline the reason.

3. Is the paragraph about making a house or apartment a home, or is it about making a space homey? _____

(continued)

4. Are there examples or reasons? List them.

_____

_____

5. Does the conclusion do one of the following? Check (✓) the answer.

_____ talk about the future

_____ summarize the opinion paragraph

_____ add an additional opinion

B. *Work with a partner. Compare your answers.*

Your Own Writing

Revising Your Draft

A. *Look at your paragraph on page 141. Then read the Revision Checklist and check (✓) your answers. What do you need to revise?*

B. *Revise your paragraph. Remember: Cross out irrelevant reasons and examples. Add helpful reasons and examples to make your opinion clear for the reader.*

Revision Checklist	Yes	No
1. Underline the topic sentence. Did you name an item that makes you feel at home or makes a space homey?		
2. Circle the item in your topic sentence. Did you say why this item is important to you?		
3. Number the reasons and examples in the body sentences. Do all the reasons and examples help the reader understand your opinion?		
4. Underline the conclusion. Does the conclusion do one of the following: • tell about the future?		
• summarize the paragraph?		
• add an opinion to the topic sentence?		
5. Put a star (*) next to each new word or phrase from this unit. Are there at least two new words or phrases?		

■ GRAMMAR PRESENTATION

Before you hand in your paragraph, edit it for errors in grammar. In this editing section, you review count and non-count nouns. Think about your paragraph as you review.

Count and Non-Count Nouns

Grammar Notes	Examples
1. **Count nouns** refer to things that you can **easily count**. To form the plural of most count nouns, add *-s* or *-es*.	• one **room**, two **pictures**, three **boxes** room room**s** box box**es**
2. **Non-count nouns** refer to things that are **difficult to count**. Use singular verbs with non-count nouns. We often use **quantifiers** with non-count nouns. *A lot of* and *a piece of* are quantifiers. *Some* and *any* are also quantifiers.	• I love nice **furniture**. • **Music makes** me happy. • Solomon has **a lot of** football equipment. • That is a lovely **piece of** furniture. • I want **some** wood furniture. • I don't want **any** plastic furniture.
3. Use *a* or *an* before **singular count nouns**. Use *a* before words that start with a consonant sound. Use *an* before words that start with a vowel sound. Use *some* (or no word) with **plural count nouns** and **non-count nouns**.	• Steve wants **a photo** of Linda. *(starts with a consonant sound)* • I want **an old** photo of my mom. *(starts with a vowel sound)* • We have (**some**) photos on the wall. • I bought (**some**) furniture on sale.
4. Use *some* in **affirmative statements**. Use *any* in **negative statements** and in **questions**. **NOTE:** You can use *some* in a question, especially when you are offering something.	• I have **some** luggage for my trip. • I don't have **any** luggage. • Do you have **any** luggage? • Do you want **some** help? *(offer)*
5. Use **plural count nouns** or **non-count nouns** to talk about things you **like** or **dislike** in general. (Don't use *a, an,* or *some*.)	• I like old houses. NOT: ~~I like a old houses.~~

Focused Practice

A. *Read the words. Write the words again. Add an -s or -es to the count nouns. Do not add an -s or -es to the non-count nouns.*

Example:

chair _____*chairs*_____

1. furniture _____

2. picture _____

3. art _____

4. painting _____

5. paint _____

6. wood _____

7. book _____

8. plant _____

B. *Complete the sentences. Circle the correct letter. Circle (Ø) for no word needed.*

Example:

I love _____ homemade Japanese food. It makes me think of home.

a. an   **b.** (Ø)

1. I don't like _____ American fast food. It makes me feel sick.
   a. a   **b.** any

2. I want _____ old picture of Chicago for my living room.
   a. a   **b.** an

3. I want to make this room cheerful. I need to buy _____ paint.
   a. (Ø)   **b.** a

4. Do you want _____ help?
   a. any   **b.** a

5. I don't have _____ nice furniture.
   a. some   **b.** any

6. Here are _____ flowers for your desk.
   a. some   **b.** a

7. I miss playing hockey. I don't have _____ equipment.
   a. an   **b.** any

C. *Correct six more errors with count and non-count nouns.*

> *Some*
> ~~Any~~ pictures of my friends and family on my wall make my dorm room a
> home for me. My roommate and I are very different. He doesn't like pictures on the
> walls. He likes a white walls and no decorations. I try to make our room homey with
> any comfortable chairs, but he only sits at his desk. I like to invite a friends to our
> room on weekends, but he doesn't like to have some parties. He only likes a TV. I do
> not feel at home in my dorm room. Next year, I need some different roommate!

Your Own Writing

Editing Your Draft

A. *Edit your paragraph for the assignment. Use the Editing Checklist below.*

B. *Write a clean copy of your paragraph. Give it to your teacher.*

Editing Checklist		
Did you . . .	**Yes**	**No**
• use *some, any*, and count and non-count nouns correctly?		
• use vocabulary from the unit?		
• use correct paragraph format??		
• give good reasons and examples?		
• include a title?		
• use capitalization and punctuation correctly?		

UNIT 8 Luck

IN THIS UNIT This unit is about lucky situations. What kind of luck do people have? When is luck important?

People often work very hard to reach a goal. They might work hard to create something new, earn money, or stay healthy. But sometimes we cannot control what happens. Sometimes, for better or worse, luck interferes. Bad luck, like an accident, can be very painful. Good luck, like finding money, or being in the right place at the right time, can change your life.

Are you generally a lucky person? What lucky experiences do you remember?

Planning for Writing

■ BRAINSTORM

A. *Read about Flight 1549. Then read the questions. Discuss your answers with a partner.*

Flight 1549 was very lucky. The plane left La Guardia Airport in New York at 3:25 on January 15, 2009. Then, two minutes later, the engines stopped. The plane hit a large group of birds and lost power. The pilot turned the plane around to go back to La Guardia Airport. He wanted to land the plane safely at the airport, but there was no time. Instead, he landed the plane on the icy water of the Hudson River. Private boats and rescue boats saw the plane land and rushed to help. All 155 passengers and crew escaped safely. The passengers agreed that they were very lucky. They were lucky because the pilot was Captain Chesley B. Sullenberg. He was a very experienced pilot, and he made excellent decisions. He was the right pilot at the right time. Captain Sullenberg has experience, but he probably had some very good luck too.

1. Why did the plane lose power?
2. How does an airplane crash usually end?
3. Why do the passengers say Flight 1549 was lucky?

B. Using a Timeline. *A timeline helps you think about important events and put the events in order. Look at the timeline below. What events from the timeline are in the paragraph on page 149? Check (✓) the events from the paragraph.*

3:00 P.M.	
3:25 P.M.	☐ Flight 1549 left La Guardia
3:27:01 P.M.	☐ hit birds
3:27:15 P.M.	☐ engines stopped / plane lost power
3:27:30 P.M.	☐ pilot turned plane around
3:30 P.M.	☐ plane landed on water
3:35 P.M.	☐ people photographed the plane
3:30–3:40 P.M.	☐ everyone escaped
4:30 P.M.	☐ everyone was rescued
5:00 P.M.	☐ passengers thanked the crew
5:00 P.M.	

C. *Read about another lucky situation. Complete the timeline about the situation.*

Six months ago, Naomi was at a park. She saw a little boy fall and hurt himself. The boy's mother did not have a car to take him to the hospital, so Naomi drove them. At the time, Naomi did not know that the woman owned a big company. The woman needed an assistant, so she hired Naomi. Two weeks after Naomi started her job, she went to the yearly office party, and she won the grand prize. She won a new bike. Now, Naomi has a great job, a new friend, and a new bike.

Six months ago — *was at a park* _____

_____

_____

_____

2 weeks after that — *went to office party* _____

_____

The Flight of the Gossamer Albatross

6 A.M. on June 12, 1979, Allen began pedaling[2] the Albatross and left the beach in England.

4 The sea was calm, and there was very little wind, but soon Allen began to have some bad luck. First, the radio broke, so Allen was unable to talk to the people in the boats following him. Next, the wind became strong, and the Albatross slowed down. Allen drank all of his water, and he became very tired and thirsty. Finally, the instruments[3] stopped working. Without the instruments, Allen did not know the height or the speed of the Albatross.

1 On June 12, 1979, the Gossamer Albatross flew across the English Channel in 2 hours, 49 minutes. The Gossamer Albatross looks like an old-fashioned airplane. It weighs only 70 pounds, and it has no engines. Its power comes from the pilot, a cyclist named Bryan Allen. Dr. Paul MacCready designed the aircraft. After a lot of hard work and some well-timed luck at the end, he won a £100,000 prize for the successful flight.

2 MacCready and his team began to design the Albatross in 1977. The first very short flights in the summer of 1978 went well, but the longer flights had problems. The team needed to make a lot of repairs and improvements.[1] Soon, the Albatross flew for 15 minutes. After the team made more improvements in April, 1979, Allen flew the Albatross for 69 minutes over a lake.

3 MacCready and his team worked on the Albatross. At the same time, Allen exercised. He rode his bicycle 40 to 80 miles a day. Then, just before

5 Allen did not see land, so he decided to end the flight. He planned to land the Albatross on one of the boats following him. He wanted to make room for the boat below him, so he flew the Albatross higher into the air. The higher the plane went, the calmer the wind became. That was good luck! Allen signaled[4] to the boat to wait "five more minutes." He signaled again five minutes later, and then again after another five minutes. An hour later, Allen finally landed on the beach at Cap Gris-Nez, France, and won the big prize.

---

[1] **improvement:** something you do to make a thing better
[2] **pedaling:** pushing the pedals on a bicycle with your feet to make it go
[3] **instruments:** a pilot's equipment on an airplane
[4] **signaled:** made a sound or moved hands to tell someone to do something

Building Word Knowledge

Word Families. Many words in English are part of a family. The words in the family usually share the same meaning, but they can have different forms of the main word. In this unit, you write about luck. *Luck* is a main word. It is a noun. *Lucky* is an adjective. *Luckily* is an adverb. All the words in this family share the meaning of *luck*—the good and bad things that happen to you by chance. Here are some examples of the word family *luck*.

Luck (noun):

*I never have any **luck**.*

*The pilot had some **bad luck** at first.*

*Good-bye! **Good luck**!*

Lucky (adjective):

*Paul is a **lucky** guy.*

*He's **lucky** because the wind calmed down.*

*He was **lucky** to win the prize.*

Luckily (adverb):

__Luckily__, the wind was calmer higher up.

__Luckily__, Paul landed in France.

Complete the sentences. Use the correct form of luck.

Example:

Good _____*luck*_____ ! I hope you win.

1. That family had bad _____. First, the dad lost his job. Then, their house burned down.

2. I lost my jacket last night. _____, my wallet was in my jeans pocket.

3. The _____ people got home before the road closed.

4. You're _____ to have a nice family and a safe house.

5. _____, it never snows in Los Angeles.

6. In China, the number eight and the color red bring good _____.

7. Nicole is _____ because her mother is a doctor.

8. Jacob and Sydney are _____ to have a swimming pool.

Comprehension

A. *Read "The Flight of the Gossamer Albatross" on page 151 again. Then, read each sentence. Write* T *if the statement is true. Write* F *if the statement is false.*

_____ **1.** The Gossamer Albatross is a small plane with only two engines.

_____ **2.** The Gossamer Albatross looks like an old, light airplane.

_____ **3.** Bryan Allen was a cyclist and the pilot of the Gossamer Albatross.

_____ **4.** The flight from England to France took 15 minutes.

_____ **5.** The flight from England to France was very easy.

_____ **6.** Dr. Paul MacCready and his team won a lot of money.

B. *Complete the timeline for "The Flight of the Gossamer Albatross." Use the events in the box.*

flew for 69 minutes	left England
very short flights	~~began design of Gossamer Albatross~~
instruments stopped working	found calm winds higher up
won a big prize	landed in France

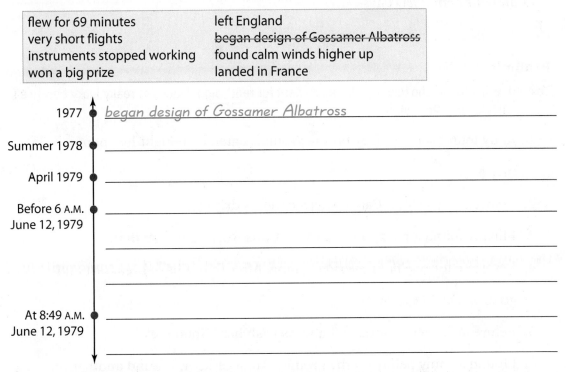

1977 — *began design of Gossamer Albatross* _____

Summer 1978 — _____

April 1979 — _____

Before 6 A.M. June 12, 1979 — _____

_____

_____

At 8:49 A.M. June 12, 1979 — _____

_____

C. *Think about the reading. Read the questions and discuss your answers with a partner.*

1. What bad luck did Bryan Allen have? What good luck did he have?

2. Which quote do you agree with more? Why?

- Thomas Jefferson: "I am a great believer in luck, and I find the harder I work, the more I have of it."

- Donald Trump: "Everything in life is luck."

3. Was the Gossamer Albatross team successful because of hard work or good luck? Why do you think so?

Tip for Writers

Time Expressions. When you tell a story, it is important to tell when each event happened. Below are some time expressions to help make the order clear. These expressions come at the beginning or at the end of a sentence. Use a comma after these expressions at the beginning of a sentence. Do not use a comma when they are at the end of a sentence.

Yesterday

Last year / Last week

After a little while / After that

A few months ago / A few years ago

Before that

Later / A week later

Now

For an hour / For a few days

Circle the first event in each sentence.

Example:

Yesterday, my friend showed me his "apartment for rent" sign. Now, I'm really lucky because I have a great, new apartment.

1. Andy found some money on the ground. Later, he bought his mom a
   nice gift.

2. Before the accident, Calvin was a careless driver.

3. I finally found a job at a restaurant. I was worried before that.

4. I exercise for one hour every morning. After that, I have breakfast and
   go to work.

5. Before my sister's concerts, I always wish her "Good luck!"

6. I found a shiny penny on the ground. An hour later, I found another one.

7. A few months ago, I didn't have a job. Yesterday, I found a great job
   at my school.

Writing a Narrative Paragraph

In this unit, you write a narrative paragraph about a lucky time. A **narrative paragraph** tells a story. The topic sentence introduces the story. The middle sentences are body sentences. They tell what happens in the story. A narrative paragraph also has a concluding sentence. The concluding sentence often repeats the topic sentence in different words. In the paragraph for this unit, it can also include an opinion, a comment, or a lesson about the story.

Step 1   Prewriting

In this prewriting, you choose your assignment. Then, you make a timeline. The timeline will help you order the events in your story.

Your Own Writing

Choosing Your Assignment

A. *Choose Assignment 1 or Assignment 2.*

Assignment 1: Write about a time you felt lucky.

Assignment 2: Write about someone who was lucky.

B. *Check (✓) the situations that happened to you or someone you know. Add your own ideas. This will help you get ideas for your assignment.*

Situations	I was lucky.	Someone else was lucky.
found something	☐	☐
won a prize	☐	☐
met someone important	☐	☐
was in the right place at the right time	☐	☐
escaped from a dangerous situation	☐	☐
had good weather for an important event	☐	☐
other:_____	☐	☐
_____	☐	☐

C. Checking in. *Share your list with a partner. Give details about the lucky situations. Ask your partner questions.*

Examples:

Who was lucky?

How was that person lucky?

What happened?

D. *Choose the person and the situation for your assignment. Write the name of the lucky person and the situation. Then complete the timeline.*

Name of the Person: _____

Situation: _____

Step 2 Writing the First Draft

■ THE TOPIC SENTENCE

The topic sentence in a narrative paragraph **introduces the story** to the reader. It tells the reader what the story is about. In this assignment, your topic sentence introduces the lucky person, or the lucky situation. The topic sentence can also introduce both the person *and* the situation.

Examples:

Topic Sentence: *The people on flight 1549 were very lucky.*

This sentence introduces the lucky person (or people).

Topic Sentence: *On June 12, 1979, the Gossamer Albatross flew across the English Channel in 2 hours, 49 minutes.*

This sentence introduces the situation.

Topic Sentence: *On July 4, 2001, I married María Rodríquez and became the luckiest man in the world.*

This sentence introduces the lucky person and the situation.

Focused Practice

A. *Read the topic sentences. What do the topic sentences introduce? Check (✓) the answer.*

Topic Sentence	The Lucky Person	The Lucky Situation
1. Oliver is a really lucky guy.	✓	
2. I was lucky to miss my train last week because I also missed the train accident.		
3. Charlie was lucky to get two candy bars from the machine because he only paid for one.		
4. James is a very handsome and lucky guy in my office.		
5. July 1 was a very lucky day.		
6. Ms. Foster's class was lucky to sing for the mayor last night.		
7. Luckily, the weather was clear for the race yesterday.		

B. *Read the topic sentences. What will the story be about? Check (✓) the answer.*

Example:

Parking is very expensive downtown, but yesterday I was lucky.

The story will be about

_____ **a.** prices of things downtown.

__✓__ **b.** finding a free parking space.

1. John and I are lucky our neighbor was home yesterday because someone tried to break into our house.

The story will be about

_____ **a.** doing a lot of fun things with our neighbor.

_____ **b.** our neighbor stopping someone from going into our house.

2. I was lucky to get the last chicken sandwich at Bakesale Betty's yesterday.

The story will be about

_____ **a.** buying the last delicious sandwich at Bakesale Betty's.

_____ **b.** going to Bakesale Betty's for chicken sandwiches every Friday.

3. Michele is lucky because she often visits her sister in New York.

The story will be about

_____ **a.** Michele's visits to New York.

_____ **b.** the life of Michele's sister in New York.

Your Own Writing

Finding Out More

A. *Go online. Type the keywords* luck *or* lucky people in history *or* lucky stories *or* [the name of your own story]. *Find information about lucky people and situations. Look for videos and images, if possible.*

B. *Describe three lucky situations or people. Write one sentence for each.*

Example:

A large truck fell on top of a man in his car, but the lucky driver was not

injured at all.

1. _____

   _____

2. _____

   _____

3. _____

   _____

C. Checking in. *Share your information with a partner. Add ideas you like from your partner's information.*

Planning Your Topic Sentence

A. *Look at your information. Choose the person and situation for your assignment. You can choose the person or situation in your timeline on page 156, or you can choose ideas from Exercise B above.*

B. Writing for the Assignment. *Write a topic sentence for your assignment.*

_____

_____

■ THE BODY SENTENCES

Body sentences tell the story in a narrative paragraph. All the sentences are about the story introduced in the topic sentence. Some of the sentences tell **what happened**. Some sentences give **background** about the story. The background information usually comes at the beginning of the paragraph.

Example:

The Luckiest Passengers

On my very first plane ride, my boyfriend and I were the luckiest passengers on the airplane. Last year, we decided to fly to Florida. My boyfriend's parents lived there, and I wanted to meet them. At the airport, a flight attendant called our names. We walked to the desk. She said, "I need to change your seats." We did not ask questions. On the plane, we found our seats, and we were so surprised. The seats were in first class! We got excellent food and a lot of space for the four-hour plane ride. We were so comfortable and so lucky.

Topic Sentence: On my very first plane ride, my boyfriend and I were the luckiest passengers on the airplane.

Body Sentences 2, 3: These sentences give background about the story.

Body Sentences 4–11: These sentences tell what happened.

Focused Practice

Read the topic sentence. Cross out the body sentence that is not about the story.

1. **Topic Sentence:** Last week, I bought a lucky coat at a used clothing store.

   a. I needed a warm coat because I lost my winter coat.

   b. In a used store, I found the perfect coat for a good price.

   c. I don't like used clothing stores.

   d. Inside a small pocket in the coat I found $20.

2. **Topic Sentence**: A few years ago, my best friend had a bad bike accident.

   a. He rode his bike on a very busy road with a lot of cars.

   b. He fell off his bike, but luckily there were no cars at that time.

   c. Someone saw him and pulled him off the road.

   d. One time, I broke my arm and leg in a bike accident.

3. **Topic Sentence:** The first time I went bowling, I had beginner's luck.

   a. My friends took me bowling.

   b. I had a really good score and felt very lucky.

   c. I like the pizza restaurant at the bowling alley.

   d. A week later, I bowled again, but my beginner's luck was gone.

Tip for Writers

Descriptive Language. In a narrative paragraph, use details in your body sentences to "show" the reader what happened. This is more interesting than "telling" the reader what happened. The "showing" sentence is like showing a movie to your reader. Here are some examples.

Tell: *I saw a meteor last night.*

Show: *Last night, I looked up at the sky and saw a bright light. It moved quickly across the sky. Then it suddenly disappeared.*

A. *Read the sentences. Which sentence shows what happened? Which sentence tells what happened? Write S (shows) or T (tells).*

Example:

<u>T</u>   **a.** I had a bad trip to Jackson.

<u>S</u>   **b.** My car slipped and slid for 45 miles on the snowy highway to Jackson.

1.

_____ **a.** Fernando opened the box of chocolates, smiled, and quickly ate the last one.

_____ **b.** Fernando ate the last piece of chocolate.

2.

_____ **a.** I was very lucky to have my umbrella yesterday.

_____ **b.** It started to rain. It rained more and more. Then, I opened my purse. Luckily, there was my little blue umbrella!

3.

_____ **a.** Kerry scored the last points in the basketball game.

_____ **b.** Kerry threw the basketball high in the air, watched it slowly fall through the hoop, and scored the last points of the game.

4.

_____ **a.** Iliana was happy because she was lucky and won the prize.

_____ **b.** Mr. Parker said, "And the winner of the smartphone is Iliana." Iliana immediately jumped up and down. She was so excited and so lucky to win the prize.

B. *Read the sentences. They tell what happened. Work with a partner. Rewrite the sentences and show what happened.*

1. Anders was lucky to catch the last train home.

_____

_____

2. Alexis was sad to miss her favorite TV show.

_____

_____

3. Mariko found a new job after many days of searching.

_____

_____

Your Own Writing

Planning Your Body Sentences

A. *Look at your topic sentence on page 158. Use these questions and make notes. Use your timeline to help you.*

1. What is the background to the story?

_____

_____

2. What happened?

_____

_____

_____

3. What details *show* the story?

_____

_____

➡

B. Writing for the Assignment. *Write your topic sentence. Write five body sentences. Include background information and details in your sentences.*

Topic Sentence: _____

_____

1. _____

_____

2. _____

_____

3. _____

_____

4. _____

_____

5. _____

_____

■ THE CONCLUDING SENTENCE

The concluding sentence is the last sentence in the paragraph. It usually repeats some words and ideas from the topic sentence. It sometimes gives a personal opinion about the topic. For this assignment, the concluding sentence might

- give an **opinion**.
- make a **comment** about the experience.
- tell **the end** of the story and the **lesson you learned**.

Example:

My Lucky Baseball Game

I am not a good baseball player, but I had one very lucky game many years ago. I was seven years old. The ball was high in the air. It came towards me. I was scared because the ball came very fast. The sun was bright, and it was hard to see. I put my hand with the mitt in front of me, and I closed my eyes. Thunk! The baseball landed in my mitt. My team was so excited. Everybody hugged me. I tried to do the same thing in the next game, but it did not work. **I'm sure the one catch many years ago was 100 percent luck!**

In the example, the concluding sentence gives an opinion about the story.

It repeats the same word in the topic sentence: *many years ago*

It repeats ideas: *baseball player, game → catch*

It repeats similar words: *lucky → luck*

Focused Practice

A. *Circle the best concluding sentence for each topic sentence.*

1. **Topic Sentence:** Last year, I bought a coat at a used clothing store, found $20 in the pocket, and gave some of the money away.

    a. I gave some of the money away because my good luck was someone else's bad luck.

    b. Used clothing is always cheaper than new clothing.

2. **Topic Sentence:** I had a bad bicycle accident two years ago, but I was also very lucky.

    a. My bicycle was destroyed, and I bought a new one.

    b. It was a very bad accident, but I am lucky to be alive today.

3. **Topic Sentence:** Iliana was lucky to win a smartphone at her office party last week.

    a. She can also take pictures, check email, and search the Internet.

    b. She was extra lucky because her old phone broke two days before.

4. **Topic Sentence:** My boyfriend and I were lucky to ride in first class on an airplane.

    a. The seats were extra big and comfortable.

    b. I will always remember that trip and our good luck.

B. *Check (✓) the best concluding sentence for each paragraph. Then work with a partner. Compare your answers.*

Paragraph 1

A Lucky Phone Call

I had a very lucky phone call last Friday. I was on the corner of a busy street. The light turned green for me, and then my phone rang. It was my friend, Sam. It was difficult to hear, so I stopped, and I did not cross the street right away. Suddenly, a large truck drove right it front of me. It did not stop at the red light. I was so lucky not to get hit.

_____ **a.** The truck was large and very heavy.

_____ **b.** The driver was not a good driver.

_____ **c.** Thanks to my friend Sam, I am in the hospital right now.

_____ **d.** That was my lucky phone call day.

Paragraph 2

A Lucky Wedding Day

My sister had a very lucky wedding day in October. October is often a cold and rainy month. My sister planned an outdoor wedding for October 21, but she had no plans for rain. On October 19 and October 20, the sky was dark, the days were cold, and it rained and rained Then, on October 21, the sun came out, and the weather was warm and clear.

_____ **a.** That lucky wedding day means my sister will have a happy marriage.

_____ **b.** My sister was not very smart to plan an outdoor wedding in October.

_____ **c.** October is a beautiful month.

_____ **d.** This is my sister's second marriage.

Your Own Writing

Planning Your Concluding Sentence

A. *Look at your topic sentence and body sentences on page 162. Answer the questions.*

What is your opinion of the experience?

_____

What comment can you make about the experience?

_____

What is the end of the story? What did you learn?

_____

_____

B. *Write a concluding sentence for your paragraph.*

_____

C. Writing for the Assignment. *Write a paragraph about a time when you or someone else was lucky. Use your topic sentence, body sentences, and concluding sentence. Give your paragraph a title.*

_____

_____

_____

_____

_____

_____

Revising your draft is an important step in good writing. In revising a narrative paragraph, try to make your writing clear. Look at your sentences and make them interesting and complete.

Tip for Writers

Sentence Fragments. Sentence fragments are not complete sentences. They have some parts of a sentence, but they are missing a subject, a verb, or both. Sometimes people use fragments in informal speech, but fragments are incorrect in formal writing. Here are some examples.

Missing a Subject:

- Incorrect: *My friend had some bad luck with his car yesterday. First, hit a police car in the parking lot.*
- Correct: *My friend had some bad luck with his car yesterday. First, **he** hit a police car in the parking lot.*

Missing a Verb:

- Incorrect: *The police officer gave him a ticket. He really angry.*
- Correct: *The police officer gave him a ticket. He **was** really angry.*

Missing a Subject and a Verb:

- Incorrect: *The police officer gave him a ticket. One hour later, a parking ticket too.*
- Correct: *The police officer gave him a ticket. One hour later, **he got** a parking ticket too.*

A. *Read the sentence fragments. What is missing? How can you correct them? Check (✓) the answer.*

Example:

Last week, had some really bad luck.

_____ Add a verb

✓ Add a subject

_____ Add a subject and verb

1. First, took my computer to work.

   _____ Add a verb

   _____ Add a subject

   _____ Add a subject and verb

2. I put my computer on top of the car. Then into the car and drove away.

_____ Add a verb

_____ Add a subject

_____ Add a subject and verb

3. Forgot my computer was on the roof of the car.

_____ Add a verb

_____ Add a subject

_____ Add a subject and verb

4. The computer did not fall off! Really lucky!

_____ Add a verb

_____ Add a subject

_____ Add a subject and verb

B. *Read the paragraph. Correct three more fragments.*

> **Smells from Home**
>
>   *am*
>   I $_\wedge$ really lucky. I live above a Mexican restaurant. I from Mexico. Love Mexican
> food and the smell of Mexican spices. They remind me of home. Sometimes
> homesick, but the delicious smells from the restaurant make me feel comfortable in
> my American home.

Building Word Knowledge

Expressions for Writing about Luck. There are many expressions in English about luck. These expressions can help you write about lucky situations. Here are some examples.

*I **happen to** have my umbrella in my purse. It **happened to** be there.*

***Just by chance**, I saw Ashley at the supermarket this morning.*

*The store clerk offered me the extra chocolate milk shake she made by mistake. I was **in the right place at the right time**!*

A. *Complete the sentences. Use an expression about luck.*

1. I sang the song "As Time Goes By" at a karaoke club. That song

_____ be the club owner's favorite song, so he gave me

a job at his club. Now I sing there every Friday night.

2. _____, do you have your cell phone with you? I forgot

my phone.

3. I was the 1,000th guest at the football game, so I got in for free. I was

_____.

B. *Write two sentences for your assignment. Use two expressions about luck.*

1. _____

2. _____

Focused Practice

A. *Read the paragraph and answer the questions.*

Lucky to Lose His Job

In 2003, Juan felt unlucky because he lost his job. Juan liked his old job. After
he lost it, he was nervous about money. Just by chance, his friend Morley called
him and said, "I need help. Do you want to do a project with me?" Juan agreed.
First, they built a small house together. After that, they built a tall building together.
Soon, they had a large construction company together. Today, Juan and Morley
have 25 people in their company, and they are very happy. Before 2003, Juan was
afraid to leave his job and start his own company. Then, he lost his job and needed
to try something new. In the end, Juan was lucky to lose his job.

---

1. Who was lucky? Circle the name.

2. What is the topic sentence? Underline it.

3. Do the body sentences:

_____ tell what happened?

_____ give background information?

_____ tell the story in the correct order?

4. Is there a concluding sentence? Underline it.

5. Does the concluding sentence:

_____ add an opinion?

_____ add a comment?

_____ tell the end of the story and the lesson learned?

B. *Work with a partner. Compare your answers.*

Your Own Writing

Revising Your Draft

A. *Look at your paragraph on page 164. Then read the Revision Checklist and check (✓) your answers. What do you need to revise?*

B. *Revise your paragraph. Remember: Correct any sentence fragments. Use time expressions and expressions with luck.*

Revision Checklist	Yes	No
1. Underline the topic sentence.		
Does it introduce the lucky person or situation?		
2. Number the body sentences.		
Do the body sentences do one of the following?		
• give background information		
• tell what happened		
• tell the events in order		
• "show" the story		
3. Underline the concluding sentence.		
Does the concluding sentence do one of the following?		
• repeat the main idea		
• add an opinion		
• add a comment		
• end the story and tell about a lesson learned		
4. Put a star (*) next to each new word or phrase from this unit.		
Are there at least three new words or phrases?		

Step 4 Editing

■ GRAMMAR PRESENTATION

Before you hand in your paragraph, edit it and look for errors in grammar, capitalization, and punctuation. In this editing section, you review the prepositions *in*, *on*, and *at* with time expressions. Think about your paragraph as you review.

Prepositions of Time: *In, On, At*

Grammar Notes	Examples
1. Use *in* with **years**, **months**, and **parts of the day**, and in expressions like *in a few minutes*.	• Ernest won two big prizes **in 2010**. • He won **in June** and **in September**. • He got the news **in the afternoon**. • I can call you **in a few minutes**.
Be Careful! Don't use *in the* with **night**. Use *at*.	• The game is **at night**. Not: The game is in the night
2. Use *on* with **days of the week** and **dates**, and in expressions like *on weekdays*, *on weekends*, and *on weeknights*.	• The race is **on Saturday**. • It's **on January 17**. • I watch football **on weekends**.
3. Use *at* with **times** and in expressions such as *at night* and *at dinnertime*.	• The game starts **at 7:00 at night**. • I like to listen to music **at dinnertime**.

Focused Practice

A. *Complete the sentences. Use* in, on, *or* at.

1. The Gossamer Albatross flew across the English Channel _____ the morning.

2. Tina's birthday is _____ February.

3. I hope the weather will be clear _____ night. Maybe we will see some meteors.

4. Joe always eats at the Lakeshore Café _____ Wednesday evenings.

5. I am always away _____ weekends, so I didn't see the snowstorms on Saturday and Sunday.

6. MacCready started the Gossamer Albatross _____ 1977.

B. *Complete the paragraph. Use* in, on, *or* at.

Violet Jessop was born _____ October 1, 1887. She worked on fancy ships.
                                              1.

The first ship she worked on was the *Olympic*. _____ September 20, 1911
                                                            2.

the *Olympic* crashed into another boat. Violet was OK, but she decided to get a

job on a safer ship. Her new job was on the *Titanic*. The *Titanic* sank _____
                                                                                     3.

night _____ April 14, 1912. Violet survived. Then, _____ 1916, she got a
          4.   5.

job on the *Brittanic*, another ship. It also sank _____ November of that year.
                                                              6.

Violet lived until she was 83 years old. She died _____ 1971. Did Violet have
                                                              7.

a very unlucky life, or was it lucky?

C. *Read the paragraph. Correct five more errors with* in, on, *or* at.

Tony and Scot spent a week's vacation at a small hotel at the beach. It wasn't a

very good week. ~~On~~ *In* the mornings, they got up and went for walks, but it was

always cold and windy. In lunchtime, they usually went to a restaurant, but the food

was never good. It rained every afternoon, so they played games in the hotel on

the afternoons. Scot usually lost. At the evenings, they watched TV, or they played

more games. On the last night of their vacation, they went to dinner at a Chinese

restaurant. Tony found a note in a fortune cookie that said, *You will be lucky at*

March. Your lucky number is 15. Scot's fortune said, *Home is a good place to be*

now. Your lucky number is 47. Tony wants to come back to the beach in March 15,

but he needs to find another friend to go with him!

Your Own Writing

Editing Your Draft

A. *Edit your paragraph for the assignment. Use the Editing Checklist below.*

B. *Write a clean copy of your paragraph. Give it to your teacher.*

Editing Checklist		
Did you . . .	**Yes**	**No**
• use *in, on,* and *at* correctly?		
• use vocabulary from the unit?		
• include a title?		
• use time expressions?		
• correct sentence fragments?		
• use correct paragraph format?		
• use capitalization and punctuation correctly?		

Index

Adjectives
  Adjective + noun, 6
  Antonyms, 42, 94
  Descriptive, 55
  Fashion, 64, 66
  Food, 42, 47
  Noun / adjective order, 66
  Noun and adjective modifiers, 57
  Prefix *un-*, 52
  Sense verbs + adjective, 91
  Suffix *-ed*, 47
  Suffix *-ful*, 118
  Synonyms, 64
Articles, 77

Because, 112
Body sentences, 89, 111, 136, 159
Building word knowledge
  Antonyms, natural events, 94
  Expressions with *keep*, 74
  Expressions with *home*, 128
  Expressions for writing about *luck*, 166
  Make + noun + adjective, 130
  Opposites, food adjectives, 42
  Reflexive pronouns, 24
  Sense verbs + adjective, + *like* + noun, 91
  Suffix *-ful*, 118
  Vocabulary log, 86
  Word categories, nouns and adjectives, order, 66
  Word categories, tools and supplies, 33
  Word families: *help*, 104
  Word families: *luck*, 152
  Word families, nouns and verbs, 28
  Word partners: *names*, 6
  Word partners: *storm*, 84
  Words about names, 13

Capitalization
  Names, 7
  Proper nouns, 15
  Sentences, 15, 54
  Titles, 71
Collocations
  Word partners: *names*, 6
  Word partners: *storm*, 84
Concluding sentences, 114, 140, 162

Controlling ideas, 70, 88

Descriptive words, *See* adjectives

Editing checklists, 19, 37, 59, 79, 99, 123, 147, 171

Grammar topics
  Articles, 77
  Count and non-count nouns, 145
  Imperative, 30
  Noun and adjective modifiers, 57
  Prepositions of time, *in, on, at*, 169
  Present of *be*, 18
  Simple past: regular and irregular verbs, 97
  Simple present, 36
  Subject and object pronouns, 122
Graphic organizers
  Cluster chart, 61
  E-chart, 126
  Main idea / supporting details chart, 101
  Process chart, 22
  Ranking chart, 39
  Timeline, 150
  Wh- questions chart, 81
  Word web, 3

Organizing
  Narrative paragraph, 155
  Opinion paragraph, 130
  Process description, 27

Paragraph
  Background information, 159
  Body sentences, 89, 111, 136, 159
  Concluding sentences, 114, 140, 162
  Controlling idea, 70, 88
  Indenting, 50
  Spacing (of sentences), 52
  Titles, 71, 75
  Topic, 46
  Topic sentence, 68, 88, 108, 133, 156
Prewriting, 18, 27, 45, 66, 86, 106, 131, 155, *See* graphic organizers
Pronouns
  Reflexive, 24
  Subject and object, 122
Punctuation, 15, 54

Researching writing topics, 12, 32, 49, 72, 92, 110, 135, 158

Revising

    Revision checklists, 17, 35, 56, 76, 96, 121, 144, 168

Sentences

    And, but, so to connect sentences, 94

    Fragments, 165

    Punctuation, 54

    Short lists in sentences, 44, 48

    Subject-verb order, 10

    Subjects, 30

Simple past, 97

Simple present, 18, 36

Subject-verb order, 10

Supporting sentences, *See* paragraph, body sentences

Tips for writers

    And, but, so to connect sentences, 94

    And, or in short lists, 44

    Because, 112

    Before, after, during + noun, 85

    Capitalization and punctuation, 15

    Descriptive adjectives, 55

    Descriptive language (showing vs telling), 179

    Explaining how, *by + -ing*, 119

    Introducing examples, *for example, for instance*, 138

    Ordinal numbers, 26

    Paragraph titles 71, 75

    Reasons and examples (relevance), 142

    Sentence fragments, 165

    Short lists in sentences, 50, 54

    Time order words, 34, 85

    Time expressions, 154

Topic sentences, 68, 88, 108, 133, 156

Transition words

    Time order words, 34, 85

    Cause-effect, *because*, 112

    And, but, so, 94

Vocabulary skills, *See* building word knowledge

Vocabulary log, 86

Word forms

    Word families: *help*, 104

    Word families: *luck*, 152

    Word families, nouns and verbs, 28

Writing assignments

    Topic related sentences, 8, 27

    Topic related paragraphs, 45, 67, 87, 106, 131, 155

    Narrative paragraph, 155

    Opinion paragraph, 130

Acknowledgments

Thank you to all of my mentors: Kerry McCollum and the Peace Corps Morocco ESL team who got me started on this path; Dr. Pat Porter and the San Francisco State University TESOL department of the mid-1990's; Carol Numrich, Beth Maher and the Northstar team at Pearson; and Kate Griffeath at the Academy of Art University.

Thanks to my family John, Emmet, Oliver for their patience and input.

And a huge thank you to Penny Laporte for tremendous support, guidance and humor with this project.

Natasha Haugnes

Credits